THE VILLA ... TH
(
PAST CENTURIES

by

LAWRENCE A. FOXEN

Cover Photograph: "The Priory Gateway, built in 1475." (Photo: Ken Clow)

PREFACE

Many guides have been written about St. Osyth Priory and the Church, probably the most famous being that written in 1871 by John Watney, Jnr., which incorporated the Will of Countess Rivers and the detailed inventory of the contents of the Priory at the time it was surrendered to King Henry VIII. All of these included the story of the martyrdom of the lady Osyth but, so far, I have not found any about the village itself, or of the manner in which the villagers lived, worked and played. Therefore, I have endeavoured to write a story of the village rather than a history although this cannot, of course, be ignored.

I have drawn freely upon these various sources but, in addition, have over a number of years spent many hours in the Essex County Record Offices at Chelmsford and Colchester and the County Libraries at Colchester and Clacton.

My association with the village covers almost thirty five years, being a resident for twenty five of those years, and my interest was sparked off by a lecture given by Mr. A. J. Brown of Colchester on behalf of the Worker's Educational Association. This was followed fairly recently by a further series of talks which again included some mention of St. Osyth.

No attempt has been made to deal with many events in the present century apart from those facts which are indisputable. This is because I realise that there are so many people still living in the village whose parents or grandparents also lived here, that it would be presumptuous of me to describe village life in the 1900's when there are many others more qualified to do so.

One of my greatest difficulties has not been what to include in this book but, rather, what to leave out to make it readable and interesting both to local inhabitants and to the thousands of visitors who come to the village each year. I have collected a great store of information but, if it was all included, it would tend to turn the book into a history of dates and happenings.

Although I have divided it into chapters with different headings, it will be appreciated that many subjects are connected: for example, the locking away of a person in the village 'çage' for drunkenness can be regarded as part of village administration of the law, but at the same time it can also be said that it was part of everyday village life! The same reasoning applies to meetings of the Vestry which had its roots in the Church, but whose decisions affected the village way of life.

I am quite sure that some items will bring back family memories which would fill in many of the gaps which are left and can only hope that those who can do so, will record these before they are lost for ever.

In conclusion, I would remind readers that 1994 is the centenary of the Act of Parliament which brought into being Local Parish Councils. This would be a wonderful opportunity for a comprehensive book to be issued to commemorate this event and I am sure that as that time approaches, our local Parish Council would be glad to receive records or notes of the past.

Lawrence A. Foxen,
Manfield Gardens,
St. Osyth, Essex.
1989

THE LEGEND OF ST. OSYTH

No story about St. Osyth village would be complete without some account of the lady from whom it later took its name.
All "histories" agree as to the main incidents of the Saint's life but they differ considerably in the details, which is not surprising for strict accuracy is hardly to be expected in the lives of Saxon saints. I have therefore attempted to combine the various accounts.

St. Osyth was reputed to have been born at Quarendon, near Aylesbury in Buckinghamshire. She was the daughter of Frithewald, the first Christian King of the East Angles, and Wilburga his wife, who was the daughter of Penda, King of the Mercians.

When young she was entrusted to the care of Elfreda, the sister of Alfred, King of Northumbria, and resided at Pollesworth in Warwickshire. One day her teacher sent Osyth to deliver a book to a lady. As she crossed a bridge over a stream, a high wind blew her over the side into the water and she was drowned. Three days later her teacher, worried by her absence, went to look for her and at the bridge, met the lady for whom the book had been intended. This lady, believed to be the Saxon Saint Modwen, said she had been told by an angel to go to the river. After praying together, St. Modwen thrice called "Osyth", whereupon the lost girl rose from the water, still holding the book.

Later after returning to her parents, she was betrothed by them to Sighere the King of Essex. Some accounts say this was against her wishes as she would have preferred a religious life. Immediately after the wedding but before it had been consummated, the King and his courtiers were enticed forth to the chase by the appearance of a splendid white stag before the doors of the palace and during their absence, Osyth and her maidens fled to a Saxon bishop who professed her as a nun. Her husband's grief was great as he dearly loved her, but he would not force her to violate her vows and bestowed upon her the locality of Chic to enable her to found and maintain a nunnery.

(This beautiful 13th century seal showing Saint Osyth making an offering of her life to God)

For some little time this nunnery appears to have been unmolested although in those perilous days many people in this part of the country had not yet adopted the Christian faith. However, in or about the year 653 (some accounts say 665), a band of marauding Danes under Inguar and Hubba attacked the nunnery and seized the lady Osyth. Despite all their threats she refused to worship their idols and at last, the Chief, enraged by her refusal, ordered her head to be struck off. After this had been done she took up her head in her hands and under angelic guidance, walked to the church which she had caused to be built, a distance of about a third of a mile. She knocked at the door with her blood–stained hands and then fell dead.

At the place where she was beheaded, a spring is said to have gushed forth and formed a stream.

She was first buried in the church at Chic but her body was soon removed to Aylesbury by her parents. Some 46 years later her body was brought back to Chic and deposited in the church, but must have been removed later to the monastery, founded by the Normans in 1118, as the tomb of St. Osyth was said to have been at the east end of the monastery church and in the inventory made by the King's Commissioners in 1539 there appears the following:–

> "Item, the skull of Seynt Osithes closyed in sylver parcel gylte with a croune of sylver gylte to sett apon the sayd skull garnysshyed with counterfett stones."

The shrine of St. Osyth is also mentioned with its "Garnisshinges in gylte plate". The shrine was destroyed after the monastery was dissolved and no trace remains of it or of the Church.

These are the main features of the legend. It is unfortunate that the dates involved do not agree with known historical details. Some people would prefer a later date which would include the Vikings, rather than the Danes, but it is beyond doubt that during the 7th and 8th centuries both Danes and Vikings were raiding the East Coast and it is almost certain that they would have located and attacked the nunnery, if it existed. No actual remains of the buildings have been found which again is hardly surprising. St. Osyth is mentioned briefly by some medieval historians, such as William of Malmesbury, and in an account of the burial places of English Saints, transcribed by Hicks from an old Saxon manuscript now in the British Museum, is the following:–

> "Next resteth St Osith at Cice, near the sea, in St Peter's Minster".

However, the Dictionary of Christian Biography says:

> "The Saint is a name and nothing more, imposed on the place to create fictitious sanctity for Bishop Richard's new monastery".

The usually reliable Venerable Bede made no mention of St. Osyth and some believe the incident, if indeed it happened, would have taken place at least 100 years later when the Vikings were actively raiding this part of the country. Indeed, Mersea Island just a few miles away was a main Viking base.

Exact details, however, are not likely to be forthcoming but it is true that legends often have a glimmer of truth in them and to this day there is a "Nun's Wood" in the Priory grounds, also a spring and a well. In the early 19th century a brass seal of the 13th century was found by a labourer in a field near Colchester. This is now in the British Museum and depicts the lady Osyth with her head in her hands standing before the door of the church with the keys of St. Peter and the sword of St. Paul on either side of her. An illustration of this seal is shown in this booklet. The Parish Church of St. Peter and St. Paul has a stained glass window depicting the martyrdom and possesses replicas of this seal and others.

St. Osyth's Day is celebrated in the village on 7 October each year with a service, either at the church or in the ancient crypt of the Priory which was consecrated as a chapel in 1898.

"The wooing of St. Osyth" a pageant performed by local players.

THE WITCHES OF ST. OSYTH

During the days of the Puritans in the 16th and 17th centuries there was a great outbreak of witch hunting and anybody who attempted healing, even the charming away of warts, was likely to be under suspicion, particularly if not on good terms with their neighbours or if they had offended anyone at some time. St. Osyth suffered at least two periods of persecution, one being in 1582 and the second in 1645.

The most well known St. Osyth "witch" was a villager, Ursula Kemp, who was accused by various persons and, incredibly, by her eight year old son who gave evidence that she possessed four "spirits" and gave their names. Her examination took place before Brian, or Briant, Darcy, a magistrate and descendant of the Darcys who owned the Priory. He lived in St. Clere's Hall, a moated manor house about 650 years old which is still in existence and privately occupied. Whilst her interrogation was at St. Clere's Hall, she may well have been kept overnight in the village prison, or "cage", the site of which is marked on a wall of a house in Colchester Road.

She was eventually executed and forgotten for over three hundred years. Then in 1921, whilst digging in his garden in Mill Street, a Mr. Booker came across a human skeleton which, when unearthed, proved to be intact apart from a fracture caused by the spade. It was then found that the bones had been fastened together by iron spikes, elbow to elbow, wrist to wrist, down to both ankles. The skeleton appeared to have been that of a woman between forty five and fifty years old and all evidence pointed to the fact that this was a victim of the witch hunts of a previous period, when witches were buried in unconsecrated ground with heads facing north. The practice of chaining or spiking the bodies was to ensure that they should never rise from the grave to haunt or annoy their neighbours.

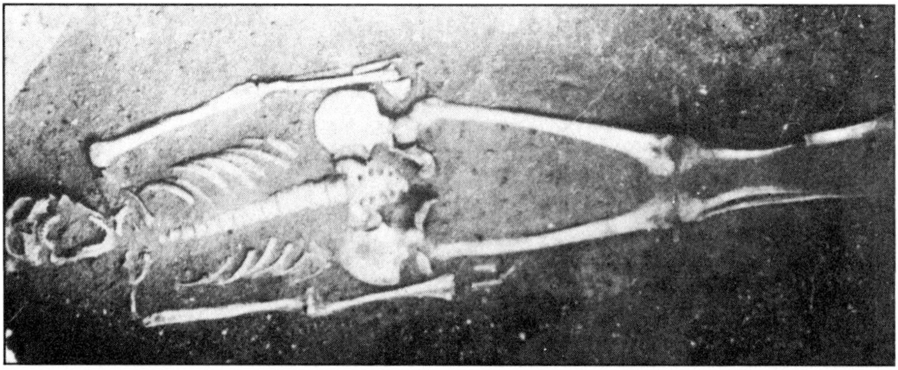

Presumed to be the Skeleton of Ursula Kemp

Not much publicity has been given to the fact that a second skeleton was discovered nearby, also with rivetted limbs: this, a victim of similar persecution was probably Elizabeth Bennett. The first skeleton, which had been taken to be that of Ursula Kemp, was taken to a museum at Boscastle in Cornwall. In recent years it was offered back to the village but the offer was declined.

It cannot be said for certain which, if either, of these bodies was in fact Ursula Kemp, but the age of the remains and the manner in which they were bound

St. Clere's Hall where Ursula Kemp was interrogated

certainly fits a time when such persecution took place and a book published in 1582, now in the British Museum, bears on its title page the inscription:–

> "A true and just recorde of the information, examination and confession of all the witches taken at St. Oses in the countie of Essex, whereof some where executed and some where entreated according to the determination of the Lawe Wherein all men may see what a pestilent people witches are and how unworthy to lyve in a Christian Commonwealth."

The book contains a report of evidence given before Briant Darcy against a number of women suspected of witchcraft.

I think it is a pity that the body, whether Ursula or not, should not have been given a Christian burial in her own village but feel that the St. Osyth authorities concerned acted correctly in refusing to pay the large sum of money requested by the museum owner, who, I understand, has now sold the remains to the town of Salem in the United States of America, a town much associated with witchcraft. Poor Ursula! R.I.P.

Later in 1645, despite the Civil War which was ranging at the time, there was another outbreak of witch–hunting, on a much larger scale, incorporating no less than twenty two women in the district. This culminated in four St. Osyth women being hanged at Chelmsford, namely Joyce Boanes, Susan Cock, Rebecca Jones and Margaret Landish. In addition, Rose Hallybread died in jail. Strange to relate, some of the accused confessed to evil doing in the hope of mercy, but to no avail.

In evidence Joyce Boanes stated that she had two imps in the likeness of "mouses" and that she had sent them to a farmhouse at Cocket Wick where one Robert Welch lived. The imps were said to have killed twelve lambs. She also said that she took one of her imps called "Rug" and one imp each from Rose Hallybread, Susan Cock and Margaret Landish and they were taken by her to the house of Robert Turner, a carpenter of St. Osyth, to kill his servant, who was supposed to have crowed perfectly as a cock, and sometimes barking like a dog. Such is the story as generally told.

From the description given at the time, it would appear that the servant was probably an epileptic.

In more recent years when land in Mill Street was excavated for building purposes, two more skeletons were found, one having the head of a spear thrust through the skull! Subject to further evidence being discovered the reader must be left with the story as it stands and perhaps sometimes spare a thought for the unfortunate women caught up in such ignorance and prejudice.

EARLY HISTORY

The village is ancient with signs of Roman occupation in the form of traces of a villa which once stood in the Priory grounds. Unfortunately the site has been destroyed by excavation for gravel. I have been told that when the sea wall was being rebuilt at Colne Point, certain indications pointed to the existence of a Roman structure which might have been a watch tower or navigational aid for their vessels sailing to Colchester.

In Saxon times the village was called variously Cic, Cice, Chice or Chic, the derivation of which is not known. At some time after the death of St. Osyth, her name was added and it became known as "Chic St. Osyth", locally known affectionately as "Toosey". Again the origin of this word is unknown. Officially the name has never been changed and I have seen the deeds of a house sold in 1969, where the property is described as being "within the Parish of Chic St. Osyth".

The site of the original village of Chic is undoubtedly the part now called "The Bury". It is generally considered that this name is a derivation of the Saxon "burgh", meaning a settlement, but it has also been said that this referred to a fortified place. In this instance I would be inclined to give credence to the first suggestion. The dwellings would have huddled around the Saxon church which was built almost certainly on the site of the present church. The fact that a church existed at the time of the Conquest is evidenced by the fact that when the Monastery was built it was granted the tithes due to the church.

Not a great deal is known of the period up to the time of the Norman Conquest, apart from the activities of the Danish pirates mentioned previously in the Legend and the fact that Vikings were active in the locality, having a main base on nearby Mersea Island and possibly a camp at Holland Haven. The district was part of the royal lands and was given by King Knut (Canute), who hunted here, to Godwin, Earl of Kent. From him it passed to Christchurch in Canterbury under licence of King Edward the Confessor. After the Conquest it passed to London, where in 1108 Bishop Richard de Belmeis was engaged in continuing the work of building old St. Paul's. His predecessor had died a leper and de Belmeis, weighed down by responsibility, ill—health and a fear of leprosy, looked around for a place of retirement and found Chic. In about 1118 he began to build a monastery under the order of Augustinian Canons, who were and still are, a preaching and teaching order similar to St. Botolph's at Colchester which was founded in 1093. The first Abbot was William de Corbeill who later became Archbishop of Canterbury in 1123.

Bishop de Belmeis died on 16 January 1127 and was buried in the Monastery. His tomb, which was in existence in the 16th century has now disappeared, destroyed when the Monastic Houses were dismantled by later owners.

Other lands in the parish belonged to Eustace, Earl of Bologne, and his name is commemorated by the existence of 'Earl's Hall Farm'. A further example of the way in which names have persisted through the centuries is that Bishop de Belmeis purchased land from Ernulph Coket and, 800 years later, the farm and lands of Cocket's Wick are still known by that name. The name

'Wick' is generally regarded as referring to grazing lands. There are many other examples in the parish of names which date back to ancient times, such as Frowick, Wyers, Welwick and Ampers Wick.

The village is mentioned in the Domesday Book of 1088 as "Cice" although the Book was really a list of Manors, rather than of villages. St. Osyth comprised several of these Manors. It clearly shows how the Conquest affected the district and states amongst other things:—

> "The Bishop holds in lordship Cice as a manor. 7 hides. Before 1066 18 villagers now 9. Always 5 smallholders. Then 3 ploughs in lordship. Then among the men 9 ploughs, now 5. Meadow 4 acres. Pasture for 200 sheep. 6 cattle. 150 sheep and 16 and 30 pigs. Value was then £18. Now £12."

There must have been some human tragedies at that time, as is evidenced by the disappearance of 9 villagers and 4 ploughs in 20 years. There are further references which also show reductions in numbers and values:—

> "Thorold holds Cice from Ranulf, which Siward held as a manor for 2 hides. Then and later 9 villagers, now 6. Then and later 12 smallholders, now 11. Always 7 slaves (serfs). Then and later 4 ploughs in lordship, now 3. Then and later 7 men's ploughs. Woodland 800, pigs 4 acres. Pasture 200 sheep, always 1 mill. Then 6 cobs, 50 cattle, 300 sheep, 40 pigs, 6 beehives. Now 4 cobs, 4 cattle, 68 sheep, 37 pigs, 18 goats. Value then and later £9. Now £8."

Frowick Hall is also mentioned separately and there are several other references to the village. Incidentally, a hide was regarded as 120 acres.

This is a remarkable inventory of a community which obviously suffered a decline in population and value.

It is not known which mill was referred to in the Domesday Book, but it must have been a water mill as windmills did not exist at that time in this country, being introduced later by returning Crusaders. There was certainly a tide mill at St. Osyth in 1382 which existed for many centuries, almost to the present day, after having been rebuilt in 1732, but although it is not certain that this was the site of the mill referred to, it would appear very probable.
In the Priory grounds is the site of a 12th or 13th century manor house and the remains of the moat which once surrounded it are still in existence and are marked on Ordnance Survey maps.

For the next 400 years the Monastery, or Priory as it will be referred to in future, continued to grow in prestige and wealth and owned vast estates in Essex and Suffolk, including 19 manors and various churches. This wealth was constantly increased by gifts from the Crown or nobility, anxious no doubt to secure their future in the hereafter. At the end, the revenue exceeded £680 per annum, a very large sum indeed in those days. Two of its Canons became Bishops and two Bishops of London ended their days there. One of these, Bishop de Santa Maria, was involved with the Barons who forced King John to "sign" Magna Carta in 1215 with a cross. A charter, given to the Priory by

Henry II, granted various privileges including liberty to keep "two "hariers" and four fox hounds for hunting the hare and the fox". This could well be the first recorded instance of fox hunting. One Abbot in the days of Richard II must have been too fond of the King's venison, for he was thrown into Colchester gaol, but later released "upon the bail of twelve persons". The sequel is unknown but I cannot imagine that the penalty would have been too harsh, bearing in mind his status. It is a fact that deer have roamed the Priory grounds for many centuries and may be seen there today.

Deer in St. Osyth Priory Grounds

On the East Coast there has always been the danger of floods from breaches of the sea walls and St. Osyth has had this problem on many occasions. During the winter of 1376/77 there was recorded a "Great Tide" and again in 1382, there was a flood which damaged the Tide Mill and cost the then Monastery £100 in repairs to the mill, the bridge over the creek and to a stretch of sea wall in Flag Creek, which protected pasture "for 70 cattle and 100 muttons and ewes".

When the great religious houses were suppressed by Henry VIII, after acknowledging the supremacy of the King in 1534, the Priory was finally surrendered on 28 July 1539 by the then Abott, who was named Colchester (formerly Withrick). He received a pension of £100 per annum and the Prior and 16 canons received pensions ranging from £6. 13s. 4d. to £10 per annum (a "Rat Katcher" received one shilling). Ironically, the Abbot at Colchester, John Becke, refused to surrender and was later hanged at Greenstead in Colchester. The last Abbot but one, John Vyntoner or Vintner, who died on 19 April 1533, embarked on a very ambitious rebuilding programme which included both the Priory and the Church and during his time the greater part of the old monastic buildings must have been taken down and rebuilt. He delighted in having his rebus (a representation or pun on his name) carved or inscribed wherever possible. This was almost always a bunch of grapes, a tun of wine and the initials J.V. The date 1527 is inscribed on a window in the Great Chamber, to be seen when looking through the entrance to the Gatehouse.

I will not go into detail as to the Priory buildings as they are today, for they are the subject of an official guide, but would mention the great Gatehouse, erected in 1475 during the abbacy of John Deeping, which is regarded by many as being the finest example of a medieval gatehouse in existence in this country; the ancient tithe barn which can be seen to the left of the Gatehouse and the archway which the Historical Commission feel may have been the original entrance to the Monastery. Not mentioned in the Official Guide are two mounds on the estate, both circular, one being surrounded by a shallow ditch. Nothing appears to be known of their origin.

Probably the original entrance to the Monastery

After the surrender of the Priory, many persons of high rank wished to obtain possession of its huge estates, particularly Sir Thomas Audley, who appears to have induced the Abbot to yield up the Priory to the King. Almost all the furniture in the house was delivered 'for the use of my Lord Chancellor'. Audley was then Chancellor of the Court of Augmentations. He did not, however, obtain possession and instead, in 1539, was granted the Abbey of Walden where he later built the magnificent mansion of Audley End.

Thomas Cromwell, who was in high favour with the King, was virtually in charge of the conduct of the Reformation as Vicar–General and Vice–Regent for all spiritual offices. We owe it to him that in September 1538, he instructed all bishops and curates throughout the realm, to place a bible printed in English and also a register to record all weddings, christenings and burials in every church. For his zeal he was rewarded with the grant of many manors and valuable estates in Essex and elsewhere, including the grant of "the dissolved Monastery of St. Osyth together with all the Manors and lands pertaining thereto, and the appropriate rectories of Chich alias St. Osyth, Great and Little Clacton and Little Holland, to hold of the King by the service of a whole knight's fee".

Cromwell had many enemies and although created Earl of Essex on 14 April 1540, he was arrested on a charge of treason on 10 June, and was executed on 28 July of that year. The estates then reverted to the King who installed Sir Thomas Darcy and visited him at St. Osyth in 1543, possibly to see for himself the extent of the estate. On the death of Henry VIII the estates were granted by Edward VI to his sister, the Princess Mary, for her life or until an honourable marriage should be provided for her. By letters patent dated 4 April 1550, reversion of much of the estate was granted to Sir Thomas Darcy, Knight and male heirs of his body lawfully begotten. He married into the powerful family of the Earl of Oxford and was created Lord Darcy of Chiche on 5 April 1550. Lord Darcy however, desired possession and not reversion of the property and the King wrote to his sister proposing that she should surrender the Priory to him. Her letter of 3 December 1552 is still in existence and, needless to say, she hastened to agree to the King's proposal. In exchange she received other grants of land. A grant was then made to Lord Darcy of:—

> "The site etc., of the monastery of St. Osyth and the great and little Parks of St. Osyth, with all the deer and wild animals within them and other lands, to hold all the premised comprised in the grant to him and his heirs and assigns for ever, by knight's service, by the 20th part of one knight's fee, to have of the King's gift, without account or any other than to the King, or his successors, to be rendered, paid or done".

This grant may have been flawed, for on 1 June 1553, Lord Darcy obtained a fresh one for consideration of the sum of £3,974 9s. 4½d. Lord Darcy came from a family who crossed to England with William the Conqueror. He died at Wivenhoe on 28 June 1558 and is buried, with his wife, in the Parish Church of St. Osyth. His tomb and that of his son and son's wife stand on either side of the altar in the church.

Such is a brief history of the village and Priory of St. Osyth up to that time. It is said that the inventory of the contents of the Priory made by the King's Commissioners after the surrender, is the most complete in existence for a similar establishment, itemising goods from the lead on the roof down to the spoons. It includes a reference to the skull of St. Osyth enclosed a silver gilt casket. The Commissioners included a local knight, Sir John St. Clere of St. Clere's Hall, still standing in the village.

THE CHURCH OF ST. PETER AND ST. PAUL

At the same time as Richard de Belmeis was commencing the building of the Priory, the erection of the church at St. Osyth was begun on the site of an earlier wooden Saxon structure. The fact that such a church existed is supported by the fact that when the Priory was established, it was granted all tithes and avowsons that were due to the church. The building may have been extended almost immediately as it was not consecrated until 1170, by William Turbo, Bishop of Norwich. It is a wonderful building and some Norman masonry can still be seen by the tower arch and in the form of a small, round window at the back of the church. This window is now blocked. The present chancel and what remains of the south chapel-now known as St. Clere's Chapel-are of the 12th and 13th century periods with various other alterations which were made in the 14th century. The present tower replaces the original and is believed to date from 1340, with additions and changes made in later centuries, the last possibly being the brick buttress on the outside of the north wall. I have heard from various sources that this buttress was added after the great earthquake of 22 April 1884 which damaged so many buildings in Essex and which was centred on the neighbouring town of Wivenhoe. However, from the absence of comments in church and other records, it does appear that no apparent damage was done or seen to be done, at that time. This is rather surprising, as according to Mr. Peter Haining in his book "The Great English Earthquake", the affects were felt 150 miles away and yet Wivenhoe, only some eight miles away was described as "devastated" and in Colchester two churches at least were damaged, one losing its spire! I have not been able to find any photographs of the north side of the tower before 1884, as they would have been difficult to take owing to the surrounding cottages. However, the Royal Commission on Historical Monuments, early in the 1900's, described this buttress as "modern" and it is still possible that this was indeed added at a later date to correct damage that may have become apparent later.

The tower contains six bells, three of which are inscribed "Miles Graye made me 1663". In 1882, the second and fifth bells became cracked owing to the clapper always hitting the same spot. These were repaired and the other three turned to avoid the same trouble at a cost of £80. 0s. 0d.

In the early 16th century an extensive rebuilding programme was started, under the direction of the then Abbot of the Priory, Abbot Vyntoner. The nave was entirely reconstructed, with a lovely hammer beam roof, the north and south aisles rebuilt and the south porch added. It would appear that the early church was cruciform, in view of the loss of a part of the arches on either side of the nave. The roof of the north aisle is beautifully carved and many people believe that it may well have been the roof of an earlier church, but a previous guidebook by Mr. Biddell states that one of the beams bears the grapevine mark and initials of Abbot Vyntoner, which would correspond to the time of the main rebuilding. I have not been able to confirm this, but one crossbeam does bear the initials "T.S." which can be seen from below and which may well have been a carpenter's mark. However, the roof of the south aisle is not to be compared with it in workmanship and does give some sort of credence to the theory that the north roof dates from an earlier period.

The planned alterations were only half completed by the time of the Dissolution of the Monasteries as can be shown by reference again to the hammer beam roof. You will notice that the ends of the beams are cut at such an angle that they face downwards. Had the church been finished these would have borne carved wooden bosses of the heads of angels or saints. If you stand at the back of the church you will see that the apex of the nave roof is out of line with the arch and roof of the chancel, alterations to which had not yet been started. Apart from the work on the tower, no further major building alterations have been made to the main structure since that time 450 years ago. Internally though, restoration has meant that wooden blocks have replaced the original brick floor and chairs have replaced the old pews.

View of Church from the South

The "new" building is in Tudor brickwork, the bricks being almost certainly made locally as there were brickyards in St. Osyth until recent times, one being in Clay Lane. This interior brickwork was later covered in plaster, but happily this was removed during restoration work in 1891. As you face the altar from the back of the church you will see two unfinished pillars which are thought by many to have been the base for a great arch. Looking at the fashion in which they were 'capped' when building was stopped, I venture the theory that they were not for an arch, but the supports for a horizontal rood beam. The roof of the nave and the top of the eastern wall had already been completed and an arch would have spoiled the symmetry of the east end of the church and roof and would be standing alone, serving no useful purpose whatever: whereas a horizontal rood beam with the usual cross or crosses would have been more appropriate and in keeping with the alterations then made. Furthermore, each pillar shows a place where such a beam could have rested. This is, of course, pure conjecture and is one of the fascinating possibilities of the alterations which were being carried out. It is unfortunate that no records exist as to what was in the mind of the Abbot Vyntoner or his successor.

The Reverend T.H. Curling, in an earlier handbook, refers to the two blocked doorways in the north wall and puts forward the suggestion that there may have been an elaborate screen with two galleries. An alternative suggestion was that the lower door gave access to the old screen and was retained in use until such time as a loftier screen could be provided, to which the door on the higher level would give access. This could in some way support the above theory.

The horseshoe shaped "sheepfold" communion rail is unusual. It is a copy of the original wooden rail which dated from around 1633, and was placed there in 1888, when the chancel was restored at the expense of Sir John H. Johnson, who owned the Priory at that time. In early days no communion rails were fixed in the chancels as the rood screens afforded protection to the Sanctuary. Communicants knelt on the floor but in some cases low benches were brought in covered with a white cloth (the hossack) and sometimes desks, at which the aged could kneel, were placed for their use. Many churches had no seats but a stone bench ran around the inside walls on which the aged and infirm could be seated, hence the expression "let the weakest go to the wall".
In the year 1549, we got our first Prayer Book in English and the altars were taken from the east end and placed lengthwise in the chancels, with the priest standing on the north side. They remained in this position, except for the five year reign of Queen Mary, until 1633. The sanctuaries being thus empty, the monuments to the Lords Darcy, who died in 1558 and 1581 were erected in the east end of the church were the altar had once stood.

The unusual Communion Rail. The late Canon Palmer is handing a newly dedicated standard of The Royal British Legion to John Austin the Standard Bearer. (Photo: Alex Bareham)

During the reigns of Elizabeth and James I, many irregularities crept in as the Puritan element refused to kneel at their communion and the position of the altars led to their being used for many profane purposes. Church wardens, for example, would use them for counting money and hats and cloaks would be laid on them. Archbishop Laud, in 1633, tried to bring order out of confusion and ordered the altars to be replaced in the east end of churches and rails to be erected for their protection and for the purpose of reverent kneeling. This order was probably obeyed in every church but this. Here however, the Darcy monuments not only stood in the way, but the third Lord Darcy, who had caused them to be erected, proved unwilling to have them enclosed away from the admiring gaze of the public, although as Lay Rector he was compelled to erect a communion rail. A compromise was reached by placing the rail where the Puritan table had stood.

View of Church from North side.

The font is late 15th century and has been defaced on all eight panels. This was done in the Cromwellian days when many church statues and carvings were destroyed. A Company of Roundheads is reported to have been responsible for this destruction, but there is no record of horses being stabled in the church as was the case in many places.

There are some excellent stained or coloured glass windows in the building, one of which, in the chancel, depicts the destruction of St. Osyth's Nunnery and her execution at the hands of the invaders. There is also one at the rear of the church which is often overlooked. It is modern but is well worth seeing. It is in memory of William Henry Slimon, M.D., a founder of Clacton Hospital who died in 1918, and of Maria Isabella, his wife, "A friend of animals and birds" who died in 1930.

The church is a "must" for visitors as there is so much to be seen and wondered about. Queen Elizabeth I, twice visited St. Osyth, in 1561 and 1579 as a guest of the second Lord Darcy and the church possesses a Communion Cup or Chalice dated 1574, which would have been used by her on the occasion of her second visit and which is still in use. George III frequently visited the Earl of Rochford at the Priory and worshipped at the church, which has a "breeches" bible believed to have belonged to him. Bessie, the Countess of Rochford, also gave communion plate to the church.

On the north wall are several plaques commemorating local inhabitants, one of them being Benjamin Golding who founded Charing Cross Hospital. He was born in the village and studied medicine as a student of St. Thomas Hospital in London. Afterwards he was physician to the West London Infirmary which he transformed and founded the famous hospital at Charing Cross.

In his handbook, the Reverend Curling refers to a broken piece of Purbeck marble bearing two incised crosses which can be seen at the rear of the church. This is believed to be part of the "Mensa" or top of one of the pre-Reformation altars. When whole it would have borne five crosses signifying the five wounds of Our Lord, one at each corner and one in the centre. The central cross played an important part in the pre-Reformation mass, as beneath the cross relics of one or more saints might have been sealed in. Mr. Curling also pointed out that on the outside south west wall a buttress-like projection appears to be Norman and might possibly mark the line of the arcade of the Norman nave on the south.

On the outside north wall of the church, inside a later entrance porch, can be seen the figure of an angel breaking the wheel on which St. Catherine was tortured. This was presumably a loyal gesture to Catherine of Aragon who was Queen at the time the doorway was contemplated. The inscription "M. R." refers to Maria Regina (Mary, Queen of Heaven). There is a mason's mark in the form of an incised cross on the north east outer wall.

In olden days, as is the custom in several religions in the world today, men and women sat on opposite sides of the church, women on the north side and men on the south. I understand that when this was explained to a lady recently, she replied, "Well, that's understandable. After all, it is the coldest side!"

So much for a very brief mention of the building but there was so much more that it represented! The life of the village revolved around the church. It was literally the centre of the community where meetings were held and religious plays performed, so you will see that the modern idea of staging plays in the church goes back many centuries. After the Reformation, attendance at church was compulsory and those who missed a service without a good excuse were often fined. Extracts from Quarter Sessions records for St. Osyth in 1665, show that "Wm. Mawdesley, Sam Cannum, Giles Cock and John Ingram were arraigned for not coming to church".

Many churches brewed their own ale but it is doubtful if this happened in St. Osyth as the Priory had its own brewhouse. The church was also responsible for law and order through the Churchwardens and the Vestry, who appointed constables, overseers and surveyors. An entry in 1860 records payment of £1 0s. 0d. for two pairs of handcuffs. Churchwardens' accounts for 1817 include the following items:—

Abm. Maskell, half yr cleaning churchyard, duty in church, finding bread, washing 'surplus'	£5.	16.	0d
Mrs. Nunn, washing best 'surplis' 4 times			10d
8 bottles wine	£3.	0.	0d
Ringing days as customary	£3.	0.	0d
For two foxes		10.	0d
Edw. Genery quarter yr keeping order in the church		6.	6d
Robt. Thorpe mending church pales		1.	0d
John Wells, blacksmith, Bill for repairing Great bell and other job	£2.	10.	0d
Master Cole, sweeping away snow		1.	0d
Jos. Page for bricklayer's wk.	£5.	11.	0d
Jas. Demaid for Carpenter's wk.	£5.	11.	0d

You will see that Edward Genery was paid the equivalent of thirty new pence for keeping order in the church. This may seem a peculiar payment but it must be remembered that it was customary at one time for farmers to take their dogs with them and many churches provided long handled "tongs" with which dogs could be separated when necessary. This must have enlivened many a too long sermon!

The expenses of the church were met by a rate fixed by a meeting of the Vestry and levied on the various inhabitants of the village who were liable to pay such a tax. The vestry was literally a room in which the vestments of the church were kept but the meetings which were held there became known as "The Vestry". They will be discussed later when village life is described.

Owing to the fact that while the Priory was in existence as a religious house it would have undoubtedly supplied the necessary Ministers or Priests for services, the church does not possess a long list of incumbents, as do so many others. After the Reformation it was stated that the Parish possessed neither vicarage nor parsonage but that "Nehemiah Rogers supplies the cure at the allowance of the Countess Rivers". The registers date from 1666. In 1682, a Wm. Fitch signed as Curate and in 1685, Zacharia Hardman signed as "Minister, Chich St. Osyth". Between these dates, in 1683, there is an entry in the register of deaths with the note "buried in woollens". This is a reminder of the fact that the woollen trade was so important to the wealth of the country that it was decreed that every person who died was to be buried in a woollen shroud.

Apart from the names mentioned above, many others occur during the following two hundred years. In 1768 Richard Willan, Curate, was the first person to show the ages of deceased persons. Infant mortality was high as can be evidenced by the fact that from 1795 to 1798, the births of 125 children are recorded, whilst during the same period no less than 60 infants died. From time to time there were several epidemics or plagues. In 1737 and 1738, Smallpox claimed the lives of 86 people with another outbreak of the same disease in

1767. Around this later date, vaccination was being introduced into the country with beneficial results.

The fact that the living was in the gift of the owner of the Priory led to some rather confusing situations. For example, the entry in Piggot's Directory of 1832 for St. Osyth gives Reverend F.A. Sterky as Perpetual Curate but adds in parenthesis "at Brightlingsea". It also mentioned a Reverend J. Robinson. In 1845 Kelly's Directory refers to the Reverend Thomas Bowsher as Curate while in White's Directory of 1848, the Reverend Sterky is again mentioned as Incumbent, "who has two small livings in Yorkshire, the benefice being exempt from Episcopal Jurisdiction".

The position becomes even more confused with the Post Office Directory of 1855 referring to Reverend Sterky as Incumbent, while as shown below, the Vestry Minutes show that the Reverend I. T. Morse was acting in 1852 and also in 1857. It may be that all this was due to arrangements being made between Mr. Nassau the owner of the Priory and the Reverend Sterky, whereby the post was filled on a temporary basis while the latter was away, perhaps attending to his "two small livings in Yorkshire".

In 1852, a Vestry meeting asked the Reverend I. Tennison Morse to enquire about obtaining two "Crossley Patent Stoves" to warm the church and these stoves may be seen in the photograph of the church interior reproduced in this booklet. Mr. Morse was connected with the church for several years as

Interior of Church showing Stoves, Pews & Candlesticks. (Note also Plastered Columns)

in 1857, he again submitted estimates for heating the west end of the church, "for the poor". These amounted to £130. 0s. 0d. He made a donation of £10. 0s. 0d. and applied to the Church Diocesan Building Society for a grant. At a later meeting it was reported that there was still a deficiency of £35. 0s. 0d. and it was decided with deep regret that "considering the pressure of the times on the farmers, of which this meeting is exclusively composed, and the already large expenditure by the Parish on the Church, they cannot feel justified in incurring further outlays".

A new Minister must have been appointed soon after that as, in March 1860, it was decided that the Reverend Jenkins should be paid £1. 10s. 0d. for the use of the churchyard by the Churchwardens. In 1863, the Reverend C. Bosenquet was the Incumbent but in 1864, the Reverend W. Langland Watts was appointed and remained for at least twenty years, taking a major interest in the school, supported by his wife.

The very first issue of the Church Magazine, consisting of one page and dated July 1883, was priced at one old penny and gave the information about the times of services, etc. and stated that, "There is an evening weekly service on Fridays at the Heath at 7 p.m. held at Mrs. Mills' house by kind permission of Mr. Grimwood of Weeley. There is now a harmonium".

Kelly's Directory of 1899 reported that a Mission Church at St. Osyth Heath was then building and would cost £140. 0s. 0d. with 60 sittings. At the time of writing, the condition of this building has sadly deteriorated and with falling attendances, consideration is being given to the sale of the land on which the building stands with the proceeds to go towards the erection of a Church Hall which is badly needed.

The Parish originally came under the Diocese of London but was transferred to that of Rochester in 1846. In 1877 it became part of the Diocese of St. Albans and remained as such until 1914, when it became part of the newly formed Diocese of Chelmsford.

It is indeed a wonderful thought that this church, first commenced by the Normans, has stood for over eight hundred years and that an earlier Saxon church existed on the same site for at least two hundred years before that.

EDUCATION

In the Middle Ages, education in a local community such as St. Osyth would have been very restricted, aimed at bright boys who might be potential priests or at the sons of the wealthy. It would have been certainly associated with the church and in the case of St. Osyth it is possible that due to the existence of the Priory, the village would have been more lucky than others as the Augustine Canons were a preaching and teaching Order. William of Malmesbury described the St. Osyth Canons as eminent in learning and a noble example to the country around. Attendance at church was compulsory after the Reformation and bible stories themselves were some slight form of education as were also the pictures on church walls and in windows. Later on, the well–to–do could afford to pay for tutors or send their children to the Grammar Schools that were being founded in various parts of the country, Colchester being one of the oldest.

A Will is in existence dated 1606, of William Arnold of Chich St. Osyth, a schoolmaster. It is unfortunate that in past days the address 'Chich St. Osyth' was sufficient, without giving an exact location and so we have no way of knowing where William Arnold lived or taught.

The earliest known reference to a school in the village, occurs in 1770 when it was recorded that the Earl of Rochford, who lived at the Priory , paid £10. 0s. 0d. each to Jas. Simpson and Hannah Cuthbert, Master and Mistress of a school. Payment was also made to a William Genery in 1779 in respect of a school and it would appear that he opened one of his own, as the Ipswich Journal of 14 January 1786 carried the following advertisement:–

This shows cottages on left, being site of early school, Bay House just beyond.

> "At St. Osyth in Essex. Young Gentlemen are genteely boarded and with the utmost assiduity and sedulous attention instructed in reading, writing, arithmetic, merchants accounts, mensuration and surveying etc., By Wm. Genery and Assistants. Terms £14 p.a. and a guinea entrance. Music and dancing are taught by Mr. Harrison."

Where Barclays Bank now stands, was a building owned by William Genery which was afterwards altered to form three cottages. This could well have been the site of this school.

I feel that the word "surveying" must have had a different meaning to that ascribed to it today. On 21 March 1789, a "Young Ladies Boarding School" opened "Fees 12 guineas per annum, to teach needlework and the English Language grammatically".

The family name of Genery is repeated over many years and in 1812 a William Genery was the Steward of the Priory Estates. This could possibly have been the same man. Later in 1835, the Parish let property which produced £7. 10s. 0d. rent and this was paid to a Mr. Howard for "rent of the school which his father built". It was then stated that the school was occupied by an Edward Genery, "who would otherwise be on Parish relief, he is so feeble". Next door to the Bank is "Genery House" which was the home of some of the family, and I have been informed by older villages that this was referred to as "The School House" in the past. The Mr. Howard referred to would have been the son of William Howard, who was a farmer at Blockhouse Wick in 1770 and the name was prominent in the village for a further 100 years. In 1877 a William Howard was an Assistant Teacher at the National School and left to enter Exeter Training College.

St. Osyth had a regular school in the early 1800's, probably starting from the Sunday School educational movement which swept through the country at that period. It is a very nice thought that nearly 180 years later we still have a Church School in the village! "Charity Schools" were being established by wealthy landowners and others and there are reports of one in St. Osyth in 1815. This may, of course, be the same school. However, in 1835, there were no less than four schools in the village kept by Ann Burgess, Sam Crampin, Ruth Ling and Mary Slowgrave. These were generally referred to as "Dame Schools" and pupils were charged a small sum, perhaps one or two old pence per week.

In 1841 there was an Ecclesiastical Census for St. Osyth which is illuminating. This gave the population as 1,583, consisting of 392 families of whom by far the greater proportion belonged to the Church. The Church School met daily at 10 a.m. in the morning and 2 p.m. in the afternoon and had 82 scholars, 38 boys and 44 girls. The school was supported by voluntary contributions totalling £16. 0s. 0d. per annum, the Church Rate was £43. 0s. 0d. and the Poor Rate was £824. 19s. 4d. The Census did not disclose the whereabouts of the school but it was most likely to have been the one reported to have been in existence in Spring Road in 1815.

Piggots Directory of 1832 mentions an "Academy" maintained by a Henry Crampin, who was also a bookseller. Later in 1839, the same Directory lists Sam Crampin as Principal. This "Academy" was almost certainly in the same building as William Genery's school mentioned previously.

Universal education was not popular with many farmers and gentry, who were afraid of losing cheap child labour and did not welcome a spread of learning among the lower classes. Feelings ran so high that in 1853 when a new school was being erected, the walls were actually pulled down in the initial stages and a high fence had to be erected around the site to enable work to continue. This school was enlarged in 1871 after the Education Act of 1870 established "National Schools" and appointed School Boards to manage them: hence the old description of "Board Schools". In 1876 and 1880 further Acts made education compulsory up to the age of 13 and in 1891, it was made free. In 1897 the school was enlarged again to accommodate 200 children (the average attendance being 150) and the Infants School to accommodate 160 children (the average attendance being 70). Between 1900 and 1918 the age of leaving was raised to 14.

In 1902, the School Boards were abolished and Local Education Authorities were established. The village school continued on the site in Spring Road until 1970 with, at the last, an average of 250 children and 8 teachers. It then moved to the present site and now caters for 350 children with 12 teaching staff. Between 1974 and 1982 the figures rose dramatically with growth of population and 16 teaching staff cared for 400 pupils. It is worth noting that up

The Old School in Spring Road.

to 1946 the school catered for education up to Secondary standard, some children going once a week to a school in Clacton for specialized subjects, such as cooking, woodwork and metalwork.

Looking at the present conditions of education it is hard to visualise the position of children in the early 1800's. The 1833 Factory Act actually limited the working hours of children aged nine to eleven to a maximum of nine, with two hours daily schooling. There were, of course, no factories in the village, the nearest being at Colchester, but children as young as five or six years old would have started work in the fields very early in the day and would have worked for eight to ten hours.

The School Log Books exist from 1867 and those from a separate Infants' School when this was established at a later date. A Government Inspector reported at that time praising the work of the school and recommending extensions and improvements, which came in 1871. The fact that an Inspector visited the school means that a grant was given by the Government for the provision of a certified or pupil teacher, based on the average attendance, examination results, etc. It was common for children to be away from school "as they had not finished gleaning" and quite frequently, "mothers have kept their children at home for fear of infection": while in 1875, only six children attended school owing to severe weather and deep snow, "They were dismissed and the school closed for a week". In 1877 there was fever in the Parish and the school was closed for five weeks.

Childrens' Class at Old School

Sewing was an essential part of a girl's education and was always taught. Complaints occur in the Log Book of the noise made by the children during class. In January 1892, a Penny Savings Bank opened with 50 depositors. School Dinners were started on 28 November 1918 by a Mrs. Cowley at Priory Cottage (now known as "The Old House"), Spring Road. Children of ten years and over paid 2½ old pence each and those under ten paid 2d. 73 children attended but many were absent due to the great epidemic of "Spanish flu" in 1918. The local School Attendance Officer, Mr. Barham, died in that year of the same illness. It was reported that deaths had taken place in the village and at Brickfield Cottages in The Street.

A note shows the war effort of the school during the First World War. In 1918, no less than 33 cwt. of blackberries were collected and sold for the Soldiers' Christmas Gift Fund. The children were paid the equivalent of one new penny per pound.

The growth of education in a period of 80 years can be shown by looking at entries in the Church Registers of marriages for that period and noting the number of persons who could sign their name and those who could merely put an 'x' as their mark. The figures are as follows:–

Period	Entries	Persons	X's	Literacy
20 years 1837 to 1857	208	416	200	52%
15 years 1858 to 1873	145	290	127	56%
18 years 1874 to 1892	146	292	64	78%
27 years 1893 to 1920	200	400	16	96%

Based on these figures it would appear that in the 1930's almost the entire adult population would have been able to write their names.

THE HISTORY OF THE PRIORY SINCE THE REFORMATION

In a previous chapter it was described how the Priory came into the hands of Thomas Darcy, who became the first Lord Darcy. Whilst resident there, but before actually purchasing the estate, he entertained Henry VIII, who would no doubt have wished to see the property which was of considerable importance, being one of four manors or estates which the King was empowered by an Act of Parliament to create into a honor. This does not appear to have been carried out in the case of St. Osyth. Thomas Darcy was created Lord Darcy of Chiche on 5 April 1550. He died at Wivenhoe on 28 June 1558 and he was succeeded by his eldest son, John, but before his death he made considerable alterations to the buildings. The second Lord, John, entertained Queen Elizabeth at the Priory on 30 and 31 July 1561, but it could not have been a pleasant occasion for her as it is recorded by Nichols that, "On the 30th July 1561 about 8 or 9 was as great thunder and lightning as any man had ever heard till past 10, then great rain till midnight, insomuch that the people thought that the world was at an end, and the day of doom come, it was so terrible".

This must have been rather similar to the great gale of 1987. The Queen did however, return for a second visit on 29 August 1579, remaining three days. Records exist of gifts exchanged between them. In 1561–2 "By the Lord Darcy of Chiche, in a red purse in dimy soveraignes, £10" and "To the Lord Darcy of Chiche, one haunche pott giult per oz., 12½ oz".

This Lord Darcy died on 3rd March 1580–1. It should be explained that until well into the 18th century, the year ended at the end of March and this is the reason for two dates often being quoted, one for the old practice and one for the later. The eldest son, Thomas, was the third Lord and was created Viscount Colchester and Earl Rivers. On his death in 1639, the estates descended to his daughter Elizabeth who was later created Countess Rivers. She married Sir John Savage and had 13 children. She had a tumultuous life and suffered severely during the Civil War, as she had reverted to the old religion which was obnoxious to the Roundheads. In 1642 a mob attacked her house in St. Osyth and completely wrecked and looted it. Not content with this they followed her to Long Melford to where she had escaped and again rifled her house. Her losses at both houses were valued at between £100,000 and £150,000 and the homes were utterly spoiled. As if this was not enough, she had to pay £16,979. 9s. 10d. to recover her lands. At this time the Priory estate fell into disuse for almost 70 years until it came into the possession of the third Earl of Rochford, who married Bessie Savage the illegitimate daughter of the fourth Earl Rivers, a descendant of the Darcy family.

The Rochfords were descended from Frederick de Nassau, the illegitimate son of Henry de Nassau, Prince of Orange. Nassau being the family name of the Dutch Royal House. Frederick was the father of William Henry de Zuyleston (a district of Holland) who was a friend of William III and was created the first Earl of Rochford. He died in 1709 and his heir was killed at Almanza in Spain in 1710, leaving the younger son, Frederick, to succeed as the third Earl and to eventually marry Bessie Savage. Thus bringing back through marriage a connection with the earlier owners of the Priory, the Lords Darcy.

Frederick made St. Osyth his main residence and carried out much rebuilding. He and Bessie had two children, William Henry born in 1717 and Richard Savage de Nassau, who was Member of Parliament for Colchester for a time. William Henry became the fourth Earl on the death of his father on 14 June 1738.

From the records which exist we know a very great deal about the life of the fourth Earl, especially as to how it affected the life of the village and this will be dealt with in more detail in a later chapter.

Frederick Nassau, a "natural" son, inherited the Priory estates on the death of his father the fourth Earl in 1781, but he developed eccentric tendencies and became heavily in debt. He married a Swiss, Catherine Rose, Baroness de Brackel, in her own country in 1797 and a Swiss room was constructed at the Priory for her boudoir. No trace of this now remains. They had four children, the eldest being William Frederick Nassau born in 1798, a younger son, John, and daughters Catherine and Ann Catherine Rose.

William Nassau inherited his father's eccentricity and became renowned for his unusual behaviour. He also accumulated vast debts, selling off large parts of the estate from time to time to pay them. A story is told of his great size. He weighed 26 stone and in order for him to reach his food, a large semi–circle had to be cut out of the dining table.

In 1848, there were two surgeons living in the village. One, a Robert Latten, appears to have resided at what is now 52 Clacton Road. The other was a Robert Welham, who, at the request of Mr. Nassau who was worried about his health, gave up his practice to become full time practitioner to that gentleman in return for the sum of £257. 5s. 10d. per annum. This agreement was revoked seven years later and the name Welham re–appears as a Surgeon in the Directory of 1855.

William co–habited with a local girl and two daughters were born. Later he married the girl, who was the daughter of the miller, but she pre–deceased him and it was her death and that of his mother in the same year of 1857, which undoubtedly would have accounted for his depressed frame of mind.

William finally committed suicide at the Priory in 1857 by cutting himself with a knife. His brother attempted to have the verdict amended to that of murder on the grounds that no knife or blood stains were to be found where they would have been expected to have been found. I understand from stories handed down in local families that murder was the opinion in the village at the time. I do not know if this is true and officially he committed suicide. So ended tragically the story of the Nassau family, a branch of the Royal family of Holland. The family names are commemorated by the names of roads in the village.

The Priory was inherited by William's two daughters who placed it on the market in view of debts of approximately £100,000. 0s. 0d. incurred by their father, although he was insured for £80,000. 0s. 0d. On 20 August 1858, the contents were sold for £89,765. 0s. 0d. whilst the other parts of the estate realised £129,920. 0s. 0d. If maps of that time are compared with those of a later date it will be seen how many local farmers purchased odd fields in different areas so that their "farms" are comprised of several detached portions.

A Mr. Brandeth, of a well known farming family, purchased the Priory and grounds for £12,000. 0s. 0d. and married one of the daughters, Eliza. Curiously, he did not live there for long but exchanged accommodation with his brother–in–law, Mr. Cross, who lived at Hill House.
In 1862, Mr. Hyman Allenby lived at the Priory. He was the father of the famous First World War General who captured Jerusalem. In 1863, John Johnson, later Sir John, purchased the estate, made alterations and converted the ancient crypt into a chapel which was consecrated in 1898. This was not originally a chapel, as in pre–Reformation days no living quarters were allowed above a place of worship. Sir John was a great benefactor to the church, paying for renovations on at least two occasions. He founded the St. Osyth Priory Lodge of Freemasons in 1884 and was also generous to the villagers. He brought up as his own child, a Miss Watts, a daughter of the Reverend Langland Watts, who was Vicar of St. Osyth at that time. Miss Watts became Mrs. Cowley and lived at 'Priory Cottage' at the time of the First World War. In memory of Sir John who died in 1909, she built the Johnson Institute in 1911 as a Working Men's Club in Church Square on the site of the Queen's Head Inn.

In 1924, Brigadier General Kincaid Smith purchased the Priory and frequently entertained members of the Royal Family, many of whom planted trees to commemorate their visit and which may still be seen. As a matter of interest, General Foreman lived at 'The Cottage' in Colchester Road. One can imagine that with two Generals in the village, they would have kept a sharp eye on village life!

In 1948, the Priory was purchased by a Friendly Society, the Loyal Order of Ancient Shepherds, and used as a convalescent home. It was then purchased by Mr. Somerset de Chair, a former Member of Parliament and an author of several books, the convalescent home remaining until 1988. During his period of ownership, Mr. de Chair has carried out many works of restoration and additionally has been faced with the problems resulting from the great storm of 1987 which caused much damage to the building and woodlands.

VILLAGE LIFE AND WORK

Surprisingly perhaps for a village close to the sea, very few of the population were mariners, the vast majority being connected with agriculture. Quarter Sessions cases from 1620 to 1669 refer to only one case in 31 as being connected with the sea and this rises to only 4 out of 47 in the 18th century. No doubt, however, many others were conversant with the sea (perhaps aiding the smugglers who abounded in the district!). In the 17th century and possibly earlier, there were wharves in the village and also behind the Flag Inn. From these, craft sailed to London and elsewhere with agricultural products bringing back coal and London "muck" for the fields.

The census of 1801 revealed that out of a population of 1,168, no less than 1,118 (including wives and children) were dependent upon agriculture and only 50 were in trade or other work. Baptismal records from 1847 to 1853 show only 10 fathers as seamen, against 120 farmers and farm labourers.

Apart from agriculture, the main employment in St. Osyth, and indeed in Essex, was the wool trade for which Eastern England in particular had long been famous. The wool industry in the Colchester area dates back to 1300 but from the time of Queen Elizabeth I a change was made from broadcloth to "Bays and Says", a type of worsted with long stapled wool which was not dyed before being exported, mainly to Portugal and Spain for uniforms, liveries for servants and to religious establishments for monks and nuns. The type of wool required did not come from Essex but from Leicestershire and Lincolnshire. It is known that women in St. Osyth were engaged in spinning wool at home, the wheels being supplied either by the clothier, the Parish Vestry or by the Poor Law Authorities. In 1650 there was a Baymaker in the village called Pordage and as late as 1760, a William Fiske was also a clothier.

In view of the scarcity of coinage in the country, these manufacturers and others issued tokens which could be exchanged for goods. My wife, whilst digging in the garden, found one issued by "Thomas Reynolds, Baymaker of Colchester", dating from around 1665. Women would have earned some three shillings per week and the wool they had spun would have been collected by the clothiers and taken to Colchester for weaving, fulling and stretching on tenterhooks – hence the expression "being on tenterhooks", i.e. stretched to the limit.

This was a great industry, and at one time 2,500 people were employed in the trade at Colchester, but from 1720 to 1790 it declined to nothing. Fortunately this coincided with a growth in agriculture when great advances were made, including the introduction of the four course rotation of crops, instead of the system of allowing some land to remain fallow every fourth year. In the village a typical farm crop would have been wheat and barley every other year, with turnips and clover in between. There were also other improvements such as drill sowing instead of scattering the seed and this enabled a crop to be hoed instead of being weeded by hand. The fourth Earl of Rochford, who lived at the Priory and to whom a later chapter is devoted, was foremost in this improvement and encouraged his tenant farmers to drain marshes and use many loads of London muck on the fields.

One farmer in St. Osyth is reported to have collected the soil from molehills and with it, to have recovered a great deal of marshland. Chalk, at £40 per acre, was spread and Arthur Young in his book stated that a yield of three quarters of wheat per acre was achieved, and that wheat accounted for over 200,000 acres in Essex, two thirds of which was sent to London, mostly by sea. The word "quarter" referred to a farmer's measure of approximately 4½ cwt. and not to the modern quarter of 28 lbs.

"A Job well done"

At this time-the late 1700's-the nearness to the sea became more advantageous as wheat could be despatched easily and cheaply to London from the wharves on the creek. Farming became very popular with many farmers buying extra fields as wheat prices rose due to the Napoleonic Wars. The total weekly income of an average family in St. Osyth, including wife and children, would have been only 17 shillings, but against this must be set the low price of commodities at that time, as follows: –

1lb beef	1s. 3d	1lb butter	6d.
1lb mutton	1s. 2½d.	Strong ale – pint	1d.
1lb cheese	3d.	Small beer – gallon	1d.

Rents were minimal, some being only 7 pence per week, and often paid only at harvest time. Most cottagers would have been able to grow vegetables in their gardens and there were no rates to pay on such small properties.

With the end of the Napoleonic Wars in 1815 however, there came a slump with heavy inflation. Prices doubled by 1820 without wages being increased to cover this. This, coupled with the usual sharp rise in population after a war, led to distress and much unemployment. In St. Osyth the amount of Poor Relief granted rose from £600 in 1784 to £2,543 in 1818. The Continent had been devastated by years of war and was in no position to buy goods from this country and this led to riots in the district by unemployed labourers.

Conditions were so bad that in 1830 there were strikes and parades of labourers demanding higher wages. At Great Clacton, 3 threshing machines were destroyed, more at Little Clacton, 8 in a week at Walton, Kirby, Dovercourt and Great Holland. The situation deteriorated to such an extent that some of the labourers declared that "they could help themselves and that they would do so". Fires were started at night and more threshing machines were destroyed.

Finally, no less than 1,000 Specials were sworn in to comb the area, 38 persons being arrested in one day. Some 56 sentences were passed, including 12 of 7 years transportation and 3 for 12 months imprisonment. The leader at Great Holland was a single man with wages of 15 shillings per week, "the best paid man in the Parish".

Agriculture began to prosper again from 1850 to 1874. In 1862 a Mr. Scragg of St. Osyth gave a demonstration of steam cultivation, this being at a time when more and more mechanical aids were being manufactured in the industrial revolution. There were usually an average of 4 labourers to each 100 acres and in 1871 there were no less than 331 farm workers in the village. At the same time, however, there was a decline in work for women. Then came the big agricultural slump in 1874 which lasted until 1914. This was much influenced by the opening up of the great wheat fields in America, with consequent huge supplies of grain available at lower prices, owing to easier distribution by reason of the increasing use of steamships and a growing network of railways. The cost of importing wheat was cut by two–thirds and consequently the acreage in Essex was reduced by one half. Prices fell from 64 shillings a quarter to 22s. 10d.

Unions-and there was a branch in St. Osyth later in 1890-managed to get wages up by 3 shillngs a week to 12 shillings, but they later fell to 11 shillings, and many families received assistance from the Poor Law Authorities. The Essex Telegraph of 23 September 1882, quoted the Drapers Trade Journal which reported that "the retail spring and summer trade .... has been very quiet owing to the unfortunate depression among farmers, and as this is a purely agricultural neighbourhood, we have felt the depression very much. Nearly all small farms have changed hands ....".

There was a large migration of younger men and women from villages to towns and in twenty years from 1871 to 1891 the population of St. Osyth fell from 1,674 to 1,439 and was even lower ten years later.

At this time, there was an influx of Scottish families in the area. Good farm land was cheap and the hardships of farming in this district were as nothing compared with those in Scotland. The descendants of many of those families are still with us locally.

Although there had been a slump in agriculture, there were other compensating factors. Land which had been good for the growing of crops was also good for growing other things. In 1832, 5 acres of land were advertised for sale "well calculated for a gardener who is in the habit of growing seeds for the London market". This was followed in 1863 by another advertisement also offering 5 acres "in the higher grounds, a light fertile loam, suitable for the growth of garden seeds, flowers, etc.".

Piggots Directory of 1832 mentioned John Hardy as a letter carrier and later in 1839 lists James Norman as innkeeper of The Red Lion and also as Postmaster. Apparently The Red Lion was a receiving house for mail which was delivered by foot post from Great Bentley at 7 a.m. being despatched at 6 p.m.

Kelly's Directory of 1850 confirms that Mr. Norman was still at The Red Lion and was still Postmaster. The Office of Postmaster or Postmistress remained in the Norman family until recent years, the last Postmistress being Kath Norman, the office being at what is now the butcher's shop at the Bar Corner. She was one of the Demaid family, a well known name in the village.

The Red Lion Inn and Bar Corner

In 1855 it was reported that an omnibus from Great Clacton to Colchester passed through St. Osyth three times a week. There were two surgeons in the village, a Mr. Welham and a Mr. Latten, the latter living at what is now 52 Clacton Road, St. Osyth.

A Directory of 1863 listed 24 farmers, 5 inns, 6 beerhouses, 2 blacksmiths, 4 shoemakers, 3 bricklayers (one was a Robert Atkins), 2 butchers (one a

Henry Norman, Jnr.), 6 carpenters, 4 grocers and drapers, 5 milliners and 4 saddlers. Listed also were 5 gardeners and seedsmen, one being a Mr. Skipper. At that time obviously the village was a completely self–contained community. The Directory also gave the information that there were 3 Martello Towers and a fort manned by Coastguards. Mr. Norman was Postmaster and George Eldred was a policeman. There was a veterinary surgeon, Henry Norman. It mentions two small Chapels in the village, one for the Wesleyans (now Methodists) built in 1853 and one in Colchester Road for the Swedenborgians, later called "The New Church". This latter Chapel may still be seen in Colchester Road, although now privately owned. The Methodist Chapel is, of course, still standing and very fully used.

The 1863 Directory reported that James Canham was now the occupier of "The Red Lion"-owned incidentally by the Cobbold family-and that "The Post Office was at Mr. Norman's". No address is given for this but in later years it was moved to Clacton Road to a building which is now gone, which stood on the site of Norman and Gardiner's offices. It was on this site in the early 1900's and from there moved to the Bar Corner shop.

The Old Post Office in Clacton Road

The 1871 census showed seedgrowers Robert Gardener and a James Cook of Mill Street with 3 acres. Jas. Newby, a gardener of Mill Street, cultivated 34 acres, employing 8 men, 1 boy and his own son. It is interesting to note that in 1899 a Robert Gardener was the manager of Jas. Carter & Co., Seedsmen and Florists, whose premises were situated behind the Kings Arms Inn. It could be that he was the same man mentioned in 1871. John West was also a seedsman in the village at that time.

By 1898, the number of businesses in the village had dwindled greatly as the population declined. Commerce continued however, mainly based on the wharf, which had been a hive of industry for very many years with shipping to London and elsewhere. In 1807 a Thomas Pullboro had a granary, a limekiln and a coal yard. A circular container holding 500 tons of coal was in existence well into the 1900's. The tide mill at the creek which had been working for many centuries under the control of the Priory, and later under the owners of the Priory, was let in 1777 to Theophilus Wood for £40 per annum and shortly afterwards was leased to Henry Ray for 50 guineas per annum. The name "Ray" was well known locally. In 1845 Mr. Archer took over as Miller and the family continued in control until 1945. In 1871 Fred Archer employed 4 men and a boy. Mr. Gilders lived in Spring Road from 1871 to 1899 at Priory Cottage until moving to Duchess Farm and was a maltster among other things. His name is remembered in the village by the Almshouses named after him. In 1871 a William Weeks was a coal and lime merchant and cement maker, living at what was, at that time, number 2 Overdam.

The Old Tide Mill

St. Osyth trade may have benefitted by the disappearance of the windmill which stood just behind the Flag Inn at Flag Creek. I do not know the date of erection but it was advertised for sale in the Ipswich Journal on 21 October 1769, and again on 17 February 1770, and was described as being "in good repair, with a new pair of French stones, 4 feet 10 inches in diameter and also a pair 4 feet 6 inches diameter: 1 cullin stone and a peak stone and a good flour mill with a large granary, with the convenience of water carriage within forty rods, where the shipping comes and goes to London market". The occupier at that time was John Lay and the auction was held at the sign of the Union Flag (now the Flag Inn) the house of William Dawes.

In 1823 Peter Thompson was a maltster and in 1831, Robert Bloomfield was a brewer. His property, which included a coal yard, was rated at £50. 0s. 0d. per annum in 1839. The mill was not in existence in 1871.

Bricks had been made locally for centuries and the brickwork in the church was probably local. Clay Lane, which had a new brickyard which opened in 1839 and had others dated earlier, would have been named appropriately after these. There must have been several brickworks in the past as in 1775 to 1778 nearly half a million bricks were ordered locally by the Earl of Rochford for his rebuilding programme.
In 1814, Shadrach Seaman owned the Brick Kiln field, of some 13 acres situated behind the wharf. On 15 January 1780, a man of the same name obtained the lease of the "White Hart", together with water rights. He was described as a carpenter. If, indeed, this is the same person, he must have been an enterprising man making his way up in the world!

Kelly's Directory of 1899 mentions names which are well known and remembered by older folk. Charlie Brett, of the stores in Spring Road, would take his horse and cart to Little Clacton each week, loaded with paraffin and hardware. a photograph of Mr. Brett and his son with the cart is included in this booklet. Arthur, one of the Norman family, was a butcher and also Clerk to the Burial Board. Mrs. Harriett Cole and a William Warner were carriers to Colchester on Mondays, Wednesdays, Thursdays and Saturdays. Miss Maria Norman was Postmistress, having apparently taken over from her father. The

Charlie Brett and his Son

wall letterbox at Flag Wharf was cleared at 2.15 p.m. and 7.30 p.m. and that in Mill Street was cleared at 6.30 a.m. "Letters arrive from Colchester and are delivered at 6.30 a.m. and 4 p.m. Sundays at 6.45 p.m."

I cannot let a chapter on village life pass without a mention of the lock up or "cage" which stood in Colchester Road, the site of which is commemorated by a plaque. It is possible that Ursula Kemp was kept here for a time, but this is conjecture. What is worthy of relating, however, is a story known and told by many residents. According to this, a villager was locked away for some misdemeanour, but when the door was opened next morning he was found to be the worse for drink and yet the locks were intact! The next day the same thing happened, he was locked away sober and when unlocked he was found to be intoxicated. A watch was then arranged and the mystery solved. The doors of the cage, although adequate, were not close fitting and there was ample room to insert the stem of a "churchwarden" pipe. In the middle of the night, the man's wife stood outside and poured spirits into the bowl of the pipe which were gratefully received by the husband through the mouthpiece! I can only say that if this story is not true, then it deserves to be so!

The Village Cage where Ursula Kemp may have been held.

Most villages seem to have had an unusual character at times and St. Osyth is no exception. In the late 1800's, a foreigner arrived in the village. I have been told conflicting stories as to how he came to be here, one tale being that he came with a band of travelling German entertainers and then stayed. The other story is that he arrived at the quay on a barge, with his brother, and decided to remain. Whichever tale is correct he became known to the village as a Mr. Simmett, or "Italy Jack". Obtaining employment at the tide mill, he rose to the position of Manager, under Fred Archer. The true story will almost certainly never be known but I have discovered from the census papers of 1871, that he was actually born in Italy and his name was "Schemmett", which would have been anglicised to "Simmitt". It would seem that he might have been born in

Italy of German parentage and so this may reconcile both stories. His son was Captain of the Bells in the church and his granddaughter was alive until comparatively recently.

It is not generally known that St. Osyth almost had a railway! This was planned to run from Weeley through the village, with the station near to the present bypass and cemetery, crossing the present Clacton Road, over the Mann Fields (hence Manfield Gardens) in the direction of Daltes Farm and so to Clacton. An Act of Parliament was passed authorising this, but the scheme was not pursued. Later, another idea was proposed: that of a tramway or light railway between the village and Clacton. this idea also was not followed up and so, presumably, the omnibus previously mentioned, continued to run between the areas.

Visitors and late comers to the village may like to know that St. Osyth once had its own Gas Works. An advertisement in 1865 called for a meeting for subscribers to raise money for the purpose of providing a gas works. The works were situated in the Priory grounds, about 150 yards along Colchester Road and provided lighting for the Priory and the church, together with a considerable number of houses, inns etc., in the area of the cross roads until ceasing to function about 1910.

Parliamentary elections were apparently quite lively affairs and those qualified had to vote at Clacton. The Essex Standard of 18 July 1885, states that a Liberal meeting of mainly new electors applauded Jackson (one of the candidates) who said, "Clacton is too far away to be a Polling Station and may we vote in St. Osyth in future?" Ten days later a Tory meeting at St. Osyth was disrupted by a Clacton farmer, named Bullock, backed by youths wearing yellow!

Another unusual item of interest about the village is that it must surely be one of the few, if not the only, place in the country with two War Memorials for the same war! One in the Churchyard and another in the corner of Cowley Park Recreation Ground. This arose because of a disagreement as to where the memorial should be placed as some villagers did not wish it to be erected in the churchyard. The Parish Council have cleaned the stonework of the churchyard memorial, but it is the one in Cowley Park which is currently the focal point of the Remembrance Day Service, held on the Sunday nearest to 11 November each year. The Royal British Legion, Men's and Women's Sections, join with other village organisations and Burma Star veterans, to head a short march from Church Square. After prayers, wreaths are laid at the memorial and the procession returns to the church for a service, usually conducted on alternate years by the Minister of the church and the Methodist Minister.

I have now given a short review of village life from the 1700's to more recent times, although not attempting to encroach much into the present century. As I said in the Preface, my residence of some 25 years gives me no qualification to do so, in view of the number of residents whose families have lived here for generations. I would however like to say that I think St. Osyth is a pleasant place in which to live, even if it is not quite the country village that it once was. For those who think there is nothing to do here, there are very many organisations from which to choose. Apart from these, including Point Clear-

and it must be emphasised that this is a part of the Parish of St. Osyth-there are two surgeries, a chemist, Post Offices, newsagents and various other types of shops, not forgetting a Methodist Chapel and a church which has stood for over 800 years.

Church Square as it was.

WILLIAM HENRY—4th EARL OF ROCHFORD

Due to the existence of domestic records much more is known of the home life of this Earl, probably the most famous occupant of the Priory since it became a residence. These records coupled with known historical facts, fully justify a separate chapter in this story of the village.

Born at the Priory in 1717 and educated at Westminster School, while only twenty one he inherited the title together with a very considerable landed property. At the same age he was made Lord of the Bedchamber which carried an income of £1,000 per year. Despite his subsequent political appointments he was more of a courtier than a politician and was a friend of both George II and George III, in whose service he remained for many years. In 1748 he was appointed Vice–Admiral of Essex and a year later was appointed Ambassador to Sardinia, living at Turin and making the Italian "Grand Tour", so necessary for the nobility and gentry. It was during this time that he first saw Lombardy Poplar trees and some years later imported some to the Priory Park. They were reputed to be the first of that species to be introduced into this country. The site of one of the original trees can still be seen in the Priory grounds.

On 11 March 1755, he was sworn in as Privy Counsellor and then became Lord Lieutenant of Essex. He then resigned his appointment as Lord of the Bedchamber, or "Groom of the Stole" as it was otherwise known, and received a pension of £2,000 a year but, whilst still holding this appointment, George II died and by virtue of his appointment, he was entitled to all the furniture of the room in which the death took place and this was removed to the Priory. I understand that none of this remains there now, but the quilt which covered the bed was presented to the Parish Church where it was used as an altar cloth and stool cover for many years. Somewhat naturally, there is no longer any trace of this!

His next appointment was as Ambassador to the Court of Spain, where he is said to have lived a very "full" life, having to pawn £6,000 of plate and jewels before leaving Madrid. As a friend of the top Whigs, and also of the Duke of Grafton who later became Prime Minister, these events did nothing to hinder his immediate appointment as Ambassador to France. Two years later he reached the highest position that he achieved, being appointed Secretary of State to George III, and it was in this position that he played a part in changing the course of history!

The tax on tea in the American Colonies was causing great discontent at that time in those Colonies and a meeting of the "Cabinet" was called to discuss these taxes. Apparently the votes cast for and against their abolition were equal, but Lord Rochford in his position of Secretary of State gave his casting vote against such abolition. The rest is history with the "Boston Tea Party" and the War of Independence to follow. So a St. Osyth man for a few moments affected world history although the sequel was undoubtedly inevitable.

Strangely, he later resigned from the Government because of their American policy and was then spoken of as the new Lord Lieutenant of Ireland. This appointment did not materialise and he was granted a pension of £2,500 a year as compensation, later increased to £3,320.

In 1781 he died aged 64 and was buried in St. Osyth Parish Church, in the same tomb as his wife who pre–deceased him. According to the wording on his tomb he was Ambassador to the Court of Vienna at some period, but no mention is made of his appointment to Spain. He could not have been in Vienna for very long as he was Secretary of State later in the same year.

By modern standards his income was very considerable. In 1770 his estates brought in £4,412 and he was still receiving Government pensions of £5,320 each year. If these sums are translated into modern equivalents they would equate to over a quarter of a million pounds annually. He had his taxes however! These in 1770 were Poor Rate £36, Land Tax and Window Tax £51, Carriage Tax £24 and Servants Tax £45.

So much for his political career. At home in the Priory he carried on the building works started by his father. To show how extensive these must have been, one of his estate books has no less than 59 pages listing the purchase and carriage of bricks, tiles, gutter tiles, pantiles, etc. for his new buildings. One entry in 1778 is for 18,000 tiles 'for the use of the Parish', a Peter Demaid being either the supplier or the carter. Present day builders and handymen will sigh at the statement recorded on 7 May 1775 that the price of bricks had risen by one shilling per thousand to no less than £1. 2s. 0d. Unfortunately, most of the buildings he caused to be erected have now disappeared.

It appears certain from the vast number of bricks ordered that there must have been more than one brickyard in the locality and it is indeed possible that some local farmers may have had some small kilns as was the case in other parts of the country. This is partly borne out by an entry "To farmer Jackson, 200 bricks for the "Pretty Thing" four shillings". This price would just about match that quoted for one thousand and would certainly not be paid for carting such a small number. The "Pretty Thing"? That was the name of a house near "The Beehive", still in existence and occupied. The house no longer goes under that name and was, I understand, the Pest House lodge where the women lived who acted as nurses.

The tenant farmers of the Priory were under an obligation to give up three days each year for any necessary work or carting required by the Earl under a penalty of 15 shillings per day. There is a note by the Steward that some refused to do this duty and preferred to pay the fine, which the Steward remarked, was "too contemptible" for them to worry about. Nevertheless, there are many references to wreckage being brought from the shore to the Priory and for stones (gathered by women and children from the fields) to be returned to the beach.

The Earl was very interested in sport and organised local cricket matches as mentioned in the chapter on amusements. He was a member of the bowling club at Dedham, and probably that at Thorrington Green, but most important for the village and indeed the whole locality, was his great interest in agriculture. As mentioned elsewhere in this booklet, he encouraged his tenant farmers to use more up–to–date methods such as the 4 course rotation of crops, instead of a field lying fallow for one year. He was a friend of Coke of Holkham

Hall who was the leading agriculturalist of his day, and paid for drains to be made for the marshes which were very extensive. These drains consisted of a trench some 3 feet deep, with a foot of gravel laid in the bottom and then covered with soil.

It would seem that in the 1760's he was engaged in the country gentleman's pastime of improving the layout of the estate, as a map of 1762 by Edward John Eyre, Surveyor, shows the "New Plantation" divided into walks and rides, together with a "Hermitage" surrounded by a hedge. These were a fancy of the big landowners who, in some cases, actually employed a hermit! No trace of these works now remain and there is no evidence that this Priory Hermitage was ever thus occupied.

The Countess, his wife, had no children of her own, but the Earl fathered at least three "natural" children: Maria Nassau by Martha Harrison and Fred and Anne (called "Nancy") by Anne Labbee Johnson who both lived in the locality. There may well have been a fourth child as the Earl had a town house in Upper Harley Street in the Parish of St. Mary–le–Bone and a record exists of the marriage of a John Nassau in 1795 in that Parish. Maria lived to reach the age of 95 and died in the Isle of Wight. Maria and Anne (Nancy) were each left £300 per annum on the death of the Earl. His son, Frederick Nassau, was born at the Priory on 31 July 1771 while the Countess was still in residence! His mother received £500 for his education until he was 21 and £200 for household expenses. She also received large sums from the Trustees of the estate after the death of the Earl, signing herself as "Anne Labbee" and sometimes as "Anne Labbee Johnson".

The Steward's account books from 1770 to 1781 made interesting reading and the following are some typical items recorded:–

Henry Cook, Gardener, 1 year's salary: (This figure was repeated in a later year and it could have been that Cook supplied his own labour in view of the sum involved.)	£206. 16s. 0d.
Abr. Southgate, Maltster:	£84. 0s. 0d.
John Simpson, Wine Merchant:	£80. 0s. 0d.
For liquor:	£15. 0s. 0d.
For oysters:	£11. 11s. 6d.
Dan Stevens, Coal Merchant:	£36. 3s. 1½d.
Jas. Jackson, for meat:	£72. 0s. 0d.
Thos. Wood, Park–keeper:	£20. 0s. 0d.
Eliza Crane, Housekeeper:	£20. 0s. 0d.
John Grant, Carpenter, 1 year's wages:	£19. 3s. 0d.
Eliza Engram, Housemaid:	£5. 0s. 0d.
Mary Peck, Dairymaid:	£5. 0s. 0d.
Dan. Wood, kitchen lad:	£4. 4s. 0d.
Frs. Eade, 1 year's salary as farmer:	£102. 15s. 0d.
Garwood, the Steward, for year	£50. 0s. 0d.
Rev. Fountain, half year's salary:	£25. 0s. 0d.

The Earl purchased 102 lambs at Ipswich for £51. 0s. 0d. and then paid the sum of 5s. 10d. for them to be driven home.

He gave £5. 5s. 0d. to the "Annual Charity of St. Osyth" and £1. 1s. 0d. to the bellringers on the occasion of the King's birthday and also his own. A Dr. Inman was paid £52. 10s. 0d. for tending servants and in 1777, £137. 0s. 0d. for further attendance on the family. The Earl's children, Frederick and Nancy, were sent to school at Fulham and he paid for the hire of a chaise to take them there, paying £11. 0s. 0d. for "Miss Nancy's entrance fee".

He also maintained a yacht at Wivenhoe at a shipyard managed by a Mrs. Wyatt and purchases from Mr. Popps' ropeyard are recorded. Nothing now remains of the peach house which he built with white bricks, or of a marble sideboard table. Education in the village was encouraged and, as related elsewhere, he paid for a schoolmaster and mistress and also paid £4. 7s. 3d. for "things for the children".

On the receipts side he sold an old landau to Mr. Woods for £8. 5s. 0d. and received £9. 9s. 0d. from the farmer, Mr. Eade, for the black colt "Sato". In 1770 he also received the following rents from his tenant farmers:—

Thomas Martin, The Great Park (now Park Farm):	£269. 10s. 0d.
Sam Bawtree, Wyers Hall:	£233. 4s. 0d.
John Barnard, Walton Hall and great tithe:	£242. 0s. 0d.
John Tiller, Lee Wick:	£188. 0s. 0d.
William Daniels, Thorp Park:	£184. 4s. 0d.
Danl. Stevens, Wigborough Wick:	£168. 0s. 0d.
Wm. Howard, Blockhouse Wick:	£158. 0s. 0d.
Wm. Phillips, Earls Hall:	£194. 5s. 0d.
Carrington Wilson, Cockets Wick:	£150. 0s. 0d.

The mill was rented to Theophilus Wood for £40. 0s. 0d. yearly with a new lease later at 50 guineas to Henry Ray.

There have been deer in the Priory grounds for hundred of years and no doubt, the Earl disposed of some of these to his titled relations. Certainly after his death, the records show that Viscount Galway purchased "16 buck of venison" at 4 guineas each in 1791, whilst William Rich purchased 5 brace in the same year at the same rate.

He twice entertained King George III at the Priory and maintained a close relationship with the Royal Family.

I think it must be obvious from the very many entries in the Steward's account books, apart from those shown above, that the village must have benefitted considerably during his lifetime as he bought many commodities locally and provided much employment.

PASTIMES AND AMUSEMENTS

In view of the hard life which was the lot of most villagers, it is perhaps difficult to realise that there were opportunities for them to amuse themselves or to be amused.

As far back as the 14th century a fair was held under a grant to the Priory, but this was discontinued after complaints that it interfered with fairs held at Colchester. Later, however, St. Osyth had a fair "For toys and pleasure" held on Holy Thursday each year. This was held along Colchester Road and later spilled over into the fields behind the King's Arms. Unfortunately complaints were made about the congestion caused in the road and the fair ceased in 1872. The day on which the fair was held seems rather inappropriate both from the religious aspect and from the point of view of seasonable weather.

The earliest report of organised sport in St. Osyth that I have seen is from the Ipswich Journal of 13 July 1754, which stated:

> "This is to give Notice, that on Monday, the 22nd of this Instant July, at the Sign of the Red Lyon in St. Osith in Essex, will be Eleven Hats, of seven Shillings and Sixpence each, play'd for at Cricket, by any Two and Twenty Men; each Man to Pay three Shillings Entrance; And the wickets to be pitch'd at Two o'clock in the Afternoon."

From the prices quoted, this was obviously more for the gentry than the

The Queen's Head Ale House where the Johnson Institute now stands.

villagers, although some would have been able to see the match. The Earl of Rochford had a great interest in cricket and his team played a match against another at Great Bentley.

On 18 December 1756, the Ipswich Journal reported as follows:

> "All Gentlemen Ringers are informed that there will be given Gratis Six Pairs of Gloves, to be rung for at John West's, at the Queen's Head in St. Osyth, Essex, on the 27th of this instant, December, by any Three Companies of Ringers (our own Ringers excluded). They are desired to meet and enter there by twelve o'clock the same Day or before. The second–best Company are to have Favours also Gratis. Every man is to pay 1s. for his Dinner, and have 6d. out of it in Liquor."

The Queen's Head was where the Johnson Institute now stands, opposite to the church.

Another report, this time from the Chelmsford Chronicle of 13 June 1777, said:—

> "Singing. This is to give Notice to all Gentlemen Singers and others, that there will be given gratis, Six Pairs of Grain Gloves, value 2s. 6d. per pair, and Favours to be Sung for at the White Hart, St. Osyth, Essex on Thursday the 24th of this instant June, by any Company of singers each company to sing three two–part songs and three catches, and to bring proper judges with them. To begin at eleven o'clock in the forenoon. There will be a good ordinary (meal) at two o'clock."

Still on the subject of local activities, The Essex Standard reported that a rather bizarre event took place at the King's Arms Inn, when on a Saturday night in May 1887, a Jas. Gosling undertook to eat 30 hen's eggs (boiled), but after eating 21 he abandoned his experiment. "This man ate 24 a fortnight since at the King's Arms and he then said he could eat more. Arrangements were afterwards made for him to eat 30. Several persons assembled to watch the attempt."

At the same time, a mile foot race took place between Claude Page and Chas. Auston. The ground chosen was from the Lodge on the Colchester Road to the "Barn" corner (presumably the Bar Corner). Auston won by 30 yards and a great number gathered to watch the race.

So much for events actually chronicled as having taken place in the village, but there were other entertainments available in the locality. A bowling green opened on 13 May 1756 at the Flag Inn at St. Osyth (then called the Union Flag), while another opened at Thorrington Cross on 11 April 1759, "with dinner at exactly one o'clock and a hearty welcome from their humble servant, Henry Aymes".

Great Bentley, with its huge expanse of green, was famous for horse racing as is evidenced by the following advertisement:

> 'To be run for on Tuesday the 10th of June 1777 on Great Bentley Green, a Purse of Fifty Pounds by any horse, mare or gelding, that never

> started for anything of that value, subject to such articles as shall then and there be produced, to run weight for inches; the horses to be entered by twelve o'clock on the day of the race, or pay double entrance.
> On Wednesday the 11th will be a Second Day's Race, and a main of Cocks fought at the Lion, to shew 21 mains on a side, and to fight for four guineas a battle, and ten guineas the odd. The cocks to be upon the Pit at eleven, and dinners at one o'clock. Folkard and King, Feeders.'

One cannot help noticing the emphasis placed on food in these advertisements!

The cruel "sport" of cock fighting was prevalent at that time and an advertisement advised that such an event was to take place in the village.

On a somewhat higher plane, on 24 August 1759, the Oratorio of the Messiah was performed before a very numerous and polite audience in St. Peter's Church, Colchester, the performance being described as extremely elegant and "everything conducted without Accidents or the least Disorder".

Apart from these organised events mentioned above, which from the days and times quoted, and the prices, would not have been available to many of the villagers, there would have been other privately arranged events such as prize fighting and ploughing competitions. There can be no doubt that the vast majority of the inhabitants (male, at least) would have found their enjoyment at the local inns, where cribbage, darts and dominoes would have been played. There were at least five inns from which to choose, apart from the numerous ale

Maypole Dancing in the Village Square.

houses. The number of inns dwindled later because of the widespread drinking of "Hollands" or gin which alarmed the Government so much that the Magistrates were ordered to reduce the number of licences granted.

People had hobbies and the Game of "Charades" was introduced from the Continent in the 18th century and would have been played in many homes. St. Osyth had a Horticultural Society, which in 1898, decided to have a Summer Show with athletics, the show being held at the school. There was also a Brass Band in existence in 1892. There would have been traditional Morris dancing and dancing around the Maypole. The village Maypole, dating from around 1840, is still in existence although not now useable, but a modern 'working model' has been made and in recent years children from the school have given displays of Maypole and Morris dancing in Church Square on or near to 1st May in each year. It is a charming spectacle and great credit is due to the Headmaster and staff of the school for their efforts.

On 14 December 1870, the National School was the venue for the annual public tea for the Church of England Missionary Society, accompanied by "Dissolving views on a powerful apparatus" or, as they would later be called, a lantern show or lecture. The apparatus was loaned by Mr. J. H. Johnson who owned the Priory and who was later knighted.

The Church Magazine for March 1886 gave the information that the St. Osyth Dramatic Society had promised a second entertainment before Lent, so

Bears and Entertainers passing through Village

this was one more opportunity for the villagers in which to participate or watch. There were also visits by travelling bands of entertainers, jugglers, etc., and these were sometimes accompanied by a performing bear. (See reference to "Binders", Colchester Road, in the chapter dealing with Listed Buildings.)

Nowadays, when private and public property is unfortunately subject to misuse, it is generally considered that this was not the case in the past. At first sight it comes, therefore, as rather a surprise to learn that on 3 February 1886, "The 59th Annual Dinner of the St. Osyth Society for the Protection of Persons and Property was held at the Red Lion Inn, Mr. Cross in the Chair". When the dates are considered however, it will be seen that this Society was formed at a time when there was great unrest in the whole country and rioting was taking place locally with agricultural machinery, in particular, being destroyed. Whether the fact that within 60 yards of the Bar Corner there were three inns and four beerhouses had any significance, it is impossible to say! What would be most interesting is to know is the date on which the last of these dinners was held.

"The Street"—now Clacton Road

SMUGGLING

For those who are strangers to this area, it may come as a surprise to learn that smuggling was at least as intensive here as in Cornwall or Kent. As early as 1557 it was reported that "Pirates" (as they were called) infested the coast of Essex and were helped by shore dwellers. Commissioners were appointed to deal with this matter. Among them was Lord Darcy of Chich and there were also four deputies in St. Osyth.

St. Osyth was mentioned in a report in the Chelmsford Chronicle of 5 April 1782, when it was stated that "Nathaniel Harvey, a capital convict for burglary, escaped from Chelmsford gaol through the brewhouse window into the garden and was caught, apparently at St. Osyth in a "recluse nich" in his house, behind a chimney were smuggled goods were kept". Somewhat naturally, smugglers did not leave records of their actions, but there is no reason to doubt that every inn in this part of the country had its full share of the trade. Mr. Bill Lilley, well known in the village, whose family have lived here for generations, spoke of how his father was carrying out alterations to his house near to the old mill and discovered, hidden away, a straw basket full of Spanish wine in bottles. Furthermore, it was drinkable!

Although I have found no other accounts directly naming the village, the immediate neighbourhood abounded with incidents.

In 1849, Brightlingsea Customs Officers detained several smugglers of tobacco and spirits, these being named as Brewer, Randall, Collison and Harris. They were fined five shillings each for having spirits on board the "Benevolence" between Brightlingsea and Wivenhoe. Others, Turner, Crosby and Simmonds, were also fined up to 40 shillings for possessing brandy, 2¾lbs foreign cigars and 6lbs of tobacco. The smack "Union" was caught in Brightlingsea creek with spirits aboard and in nearby Alresford creek the smack "Good Agreement" was detained with Hollands (gin) and tobacco aboard. Going slightly further afield, the local villages of Kirby-le-Soken and Salcot on Hamford Waters on the Blackwater were the chief landing places and horses and donkeys were kept there in large numbers for the conveyance of the trade, there being a constant fair or auction of contraband articles from where they were distributed to Maldon, Colchester, Chelmsford and even London.

It was a profitable occupation and in around 1825, smugglers required one successful run out of three to make it pay, the economics being as follows:–

Cost of brandy on Continent	16s. 0d. a tub of 4 gallons
Sea transport	16s. 0d.
Cost of land transport	8s. 0d.
Total:	40s. 0d (£2. 0s. 0d.)

This would reach a market price of £7. 4s. 0d. on which there would normally have been a duty of £4. 10s. 0d.

It is difficult to realise the size of the operations. In 1777 it was reported that at Holland Lough, in the Parish of Thorpe le Soken, 120 tubs of gin and

1,600lbs weight of tea were landed and in the following year a further 200 tubs and 2,000lbs weight of tea also came ashore. Smugglers' vessels were well armed and manned and on at least one occasion they actually captured a Revenue cutter. The story of smuggling in Essex and Suffolk is fascinating but much of it is rather away from our immediate locality. In at least one case it brought its own punishment. In 1782, Joseph Clark assisted with about 50 others in the conveyance of some casks of Geneva gin and one of them being left for their reward, he became so intoxicated that soon afterwards he died!

In the Parish churchyard at St. Osyth there is the grave of a man thought to have been a smuggler killed by the Revenue Authorities. The grave was marked with a skull and crossbones but is now in a bad condition and difficult to locate.

Another view of Tide Mill and Wharf.

VILLAGE ADMINISTRATION

It has been said that up to the early 1800's, villages and parishes were virtually self controlled. To a very large extent this was the case but the control was not exercised by the villagers, but by the 'gentry', well-to-do farmers and by Magistrates and this was true of the whole country. Responsibility for the relief of the poor remained with the local Overseers and most villages had their own workhouse. The workhouse at St. Osyth was in Daltes Lane and parts of it can be seen to this day. The village also had a 'Pest House' at Chisbon Heath the equivalent of the old isolation hospital. Strangers to the village were not encouraged and were hastened on their way, sometimes being given essentials if they were carrying a "pass" from their local community.

The laws governing the relief of the poor were based on the Poor Law Act of 1601 and hardly changed for over 200 years from that date. In 1776 the cost of such relief in St. Osyth was £400. 0s. 0d. in 1784, £600. 0s. 0d. and then surged to no less than £2,543. 0s. 0d. in 1818 when distress and discontent were rampant throughout the country as a result of the Napoleonic Wars.

The following extracts from St. Osyth Poor Law Records in the 1760's may be of interest:—

	£	s.	d.
Clothing Rob Alston at the expiration of apprenticeship	2.	2.	0.
2 yds of baiz for shrowd for late Wid. Webb		4.	0.
Nurses for wid. Webb		6.	6.
Beer for burial		1.	0.
Thomas Inman, Doctor, attending the poor	4.	0.	0.
Rent of the Pest House	1.	10.	6.
¼ lb tobacco for Widows Thorpe & Spindley			3½.
Spindley's cloathes mending		2.	0.
Six weeks, shaving Spindley			6.
Jas. Bennett keeping Clark's child 13 weeks		19.	6.
Collection for poor out of House, 4 weeks	5.	16.	0.
Mrs. Fine's bill for the stranger that had small pox	1.	5.	3.
Timothy Rainham, setting up a bed for ditto			6.
To Dame Mash for ditto	1.	13.	6.
Board for a nurse 3 weeks		6.	9.
Expenses on the road with			

	£	s.	d.
Pr. Pattens for girl Cape		1.	0.
To a wheel & reel		3.	0.
Pint of beer, for Richard Jones			1.
Bill for Family with smallpox	3.	0.	10.
Milk, butter & eggs for them		9.	7.
Meat for ditto	1.	18.	2.
Children in workhouse cash for fairing		3.	3.
Binding boy Carter	4.	14.	10.
Wm. Diaper's hospital bill	7.	1.	10.
Carting wood to pesthouse on the heath		1.	6.
Carting bricks to Work house well & digging it		12.	0.
John Lilly, carting coals		4.	9.
Beer for Bearers at Wid. Thorp's burial		1.	0.
Pint of wine for Thomas Dixey			4.
2 pr. of girl's stays		10.	9.
Coffin for Ann Burch		7.	0.
Chaldron of coals		6.	1.
Sam Knock for the girl Webb 26 weeks	2.	18.	6.

the stranger when carried home	2. 6.	Parish meeting at Copsey's (This was the Red Lion)	5. 0.

There are many other items, too-numerous to be included here, but those shown indicate the various activities and responsibilities of the Overseers and the Parish. For example, the boy Carter was apprenticed and another boy was fitted out with clothes at the end of his apprenticeship. Spindley was obviously an inmate of the workhouse receiving tobacco, being shaved and having clothes mended, although I cannot feel that he was the Jas. Spindley nursing the smallpox victim! Incidentally, the items regarding this man are interesting. He was found a bed, cared for, nursing was provided and at last he was escorted to his parish. A human touch was the money found for the children for "fairing". I wonder if it was for the fair which was held in Colchester Road up to 1872. In 1766, Dr. Inman was paid £4. 4s. 0d. for "cure of fracture upon the leg of Mr. Kendall's boy of Elmstead". St. Osyth appears to have always had a doctor and there are records of local villages, such as Little Clacton and Great Bentley, paying for his services.

To illustrate even further the activities of the Overseers, between 1734 and 1762, no less than 110 agreements were made for the boarding out of children or apprenticing them. Some were even apprenticed to surgeons (of whom the village always seemed to have at least two) and another resolution was that the parish should pay for a boy to be taught the violin! I wonder what the story was behind this? What happened to him? Did the village produce a musical genius, as there must have been some talent apparent for the often presumed hard hearted Overseers to have recommended such a gesture.

As will be seen from the above quoted expenses, the parish had to maintain a Pest House, or what we would later call an Isolation Hospital. There was certainly one in 1760 and it was in use in 1814, most probably up to the coming into operation of the Poor Law Act of 1834, when the Tendring Union would have provided a hospital for the whole district.

It can clearly be seen however that the affairs of the village were very much under the control of the village, albeit through Overseers and others, who would, however, be local men.

It is somewhat difficult to make a distinction between village administration and village life and work. The following items could be said to fit into either category. The office of Inspector of Weights and Measures dates back very many years and reports of their visits to St. Osyth still remain. For example, a Robert Church visited the village on 26 June 1765 and made the following report:—

Wm. Hayton, Shopkeeper.	M. Bond, Innkeeper.	Ab. Turner, Shopkeeper.
Martin Oliver, Innkeeper.	Hannah Pine, Shopkeeper.	Alice Salmon, Innkeeper.
Theophilus Wood, Miller.	George Jackson, Butcher.	John Lay, Miller.
Williamson, Baker.	Jn. Cooper, Innholder.	

All marked "good".

In 1769 however, the same Inspector reported that "John Matthew, Shopkeeper and dealer in flour, one pair of false scales wanting of a true balance of 4oz. One 2lb lead weight wanting ¾oz. One pound lead weight wanting a qr. of oz."

Further visits were paid in 1774 and 1785, which were all marked "good". Descriptions changed in many cases. Innkeepers appeared to be described as "Victuallers" and there were no less than nine Chandlers. Jackson's still remained as Butchers, although it appeared that the son had taken over. W. Holt was the miller.

The Reform Act of 1832, which gave votes to more people, and the Poor Law Act of 1834, changed this situation greatly in many ways, although control still remained in the same hands, as appointments to such offices as Overseers, Constables, Surveyors, etc., still had to be approved by the local Magistrates. It did mean however, that some villages were no longer considered as separate entities, but were now linked to other areas for administration purposes. This was particularly the case with the "new" Poor Law. The new Act revised the ancient Act of 1601 and established groups of towns and villages into "Unions", each under the control of an elected Board of Guardians. The Unions were directly charged with the relief of the poor, either by the granting of food or money or, alternatively if the occasion demanded it, by taking individuals into the workhouse. They also, and this was important, had a statutory duty to educate children under their care, to adopt them if necessary and in, due course, to find them work, often by apprenticeships.

St. Osyth was included in the Tendring Union and supplied two local men to act as Guardians within that Union. The first two gentlemen being Thomas Fisher and Abraham Carter. The new Unions took over the workhouse at St. Osyth and an entry in the Vestry Minute Book on 21 June 1839 records the decision, "to consent to the Guardians of the Poor of the said (Tendring) Union, selling the premises described in the margin hereof under the provisions of the Act etc."

The entry in the margin was as follows:

> "A certain building now used and occupied as the parish Workhouse with the yards and appurtenances therewith belonging and a Meadow adjoining containing altogether one acre two roods and thirty seven perches, being copyhold of the Manor of St. Osyth situate in the said parish and subject to an annual quit rent of Eight Pence."

This seems to indicate that although the Union was empowered to take over the property of the parish used for Poor Law purposes, the consent of the parish was still needed, as legal owners, for the sale of the property by the Unions. No mention was made of the Pest House as this was previously only rented.

Once each year a meeting was held, comprising "the Rate Payers of the said Parish and owners of Property therein entitled to vote", in order to appoint Guardians, Churchwardens, Overseers, Surveyors, Assessors and Constables for the ensuing year. Of all these appointments the least popular was that of

Constable. Not only were they responsible for law and order, but they were also unpaid. It was possible to avoid this duty if a substitute could be provided and this often occurred, the substitute being paid by the person originally chosen. As a matter of interest, the names of those submitted to the Magistrates in 1835 were: B. Baker, B. Jaggard, Jas Cook, Henry Norman, Wm Sloughborrow, Jas Dermaid and Jas Fisher. Descendants of some of these persons still live in the village.

The yearly meetings became known as "Vestry" meetings as they were usually held in the church Vestry. On some occasions, however, it is recorded that they were held in the Red Lion Inn! Decisions made were subject to control by magistrates, except when fixing a rate for repairs to the church, when necessary, and in 1842 a rate of two pence in the pound was passed for dealing with the north aisle. A few years later a rate was passed for repairs to the south aisle. This Church Rate would probably now be very unpopular, but it must be remembered that the rate was levied only on those people who owned property with a rateable value of £6. 0s. 0d. or over and did not affect the average villager. It is only because of the work of the Vestries and the care they took of the churches that so many have survived to the present day and since 1871, when the Church Rates were abolished, the structure of most churches has suffered severely due to the loss of this rate.

In August 1856, a meeting was called "for the purpose of considering the propriety of making a public sewer in the village of St. Osyth". Recently in Spring Road, excavations revealed this sewer, some 12 to 15 feet down.

In 1854 the Home Secretary informed Mr. Fearis, one of the Churchwardens, that the churchyard would shortly have to be discontinued as a burial ground. Mr. Demaid offered to sell a piece of land, in extent one rood, 16 perches for the sum of £225. 0s. 0d., and a petition was presented to the Home Secretary informing him of this and most respectfully asking him to rescind his decision. This piece of land was in the south east corner of the churchyard, but a Government Inspector rejected this solution as the land was "too contiguous" to the school. Mr. W.T. Nassau, the owner of the Priory, apparently offered an acre of land from the Warren Field adjoining the school. I have found no information as to why this came to nothing, but a resolution was passed, thanking him for his kindness and asking him if he would take into account the very large expense to which the parish would be put, if they were obliged to go beyond the village to purchase land. However, at a meeting of the Vestry on 10 October 1854, it was proposed and agreed that the parish form a Burial Board and the Board were soon in action, as nine days later they were authorised to purchase from Mr. William Carrington Simpson (one of the members of the Vestry), "a certain field, piece or parcel of Land situate within the said Parish adjoining and on the left hand side of the road leading from the said Parish exclusive of timber for the purpose of forming a Burial Ground for the use of this Parish under the Burial Act etc.".

In the following month it was unanimously agreed that the Burial Board be authorised to expend a sum not exceeding £1,000 0s. 0d. for the purchasing and laying out of the intended Burial Ground, erecting the necessary chapels, Dead

House and fences and defraying such other charges that might be incurred. In view of these resolutions, it is hard to understand why they were repeated again at meetings in March of the following year, when a notice was read regarding the closure of the churchyard, a proposal was made to purchase the land from Mr. Simpson for £300. 0s. 0d. and authority given to the expenditure of £1,000. 0s. 0d. Later in the year a further £100. 0s. 0d. was authorised. Possibly the provisions of the Act regarding Burial Boards had not been complied with to the letter and it was felt necessary for the whole procedure to be repeated. The Minutes of the meeting a month earlier closed with the entry "Resolved that this meeting now adjourn for business to the Lion Inn". I trust that this was not the cause of the confusion!

From then on, the business of the Vestry continued dealing mainly with electing members of the Burial Board, Guardians and Parish Officers and, occasionally, voting on a rate for the church repairs or for other village necessities. As a matter of interest, the first person to be buried in the new burial ground in July 1855, was an unknown man, "washed up on the shore".

Looking ahead from this period, a further piece of land was purchased in 1922 for an extension of the burial ground and this was consecrated by the Bishop of Colchester on 26 September 1988. It is amusing to relate that when the two chapels were originally erected, a wall was actually built between them, so that the "dissenters", that is any person not belonging to the Established Church, should not impinge, even when dead, onto the other portion. The wall has long since disappeared but traces of the foundations are still discernable. The irony was that for five years after the cemetery opened, no dissenter had the grace to die (or possibly, they were too full of grace) and the idea was seriously contemplated of selling off that portion. Eventually however, someone obliged and the idea was abandoned. The old bier on which the coffins were carried to the grave on the shoulders of two or more bearers is still in existence and preserved.

The passing of further Acts in 1877 and 1885 gave the vote to more people of different classes and the work of the Vestry gradually diminished, being replaced in due course by Parochial Church Councils (for church affairs) and in 1894, an Act was passed bringing into being local Parish Councils. St. Osyth Parish Council thus approaches its centenary and controls many aspects of village life, such as responsibility for the Burial Board, receiving and advising on local planning applications, making precepts for local rates, etc. They are Trustees for Cowley Park, the village recreation and sports field and although under the control of Tendring District Council and, through them, the Essex County Council, retain considerable powers and responsibilities.

I think we should pay tribute to our Parish Council members, who, despite their possibly differing political opinions, appear to act in the best interests of the community.

This is a short account of what may be called Village Local Government. There is far too much detail to be included in a booklet of this size but it is hoped it will give some idea of "management" in St. Osyth during the past two centuries.

CHARITABLE ENDOWMENTS IN ST. OSYTH

Mention must be made of the "Charities" in St. Osyth, which are under the control of village Trustees, of whom the Parish Vicar is an ex-officio member.

One charity, at least, is ancient, dating from the early 1600's but nothing is known of the original founder. It was referred to as "The Unknown Donor's Charity" and comprised approximately five acres of land on the heath near Weeley, known as "Town Fields". Formerly it also included the Round House Cottages, consisting of three and four tenants in The Street (now Clacton Road) whose rent was used for the upkeep of the Almshouses. The exact situation of these cottages is not now known but the Vestry Minutes for 1840 record a resolution that the property be sold by auction by Messrs. Cook in June of that year, the proceeds to be devoted to the repair of the Almshouses.

"Banyard's Charity", formerly known as "The Widow's Gift", was made up of land at Brazier's Farm and dates from 1862, producing an annual income which allowed for some 52 shillings-£2.60 in modern currency-to be divided amongst widows who were not on Parish Relief. This worked out at about 25 new pence per person each year and continued until 1965 when it was amalgamated with the "Unknown Donor's Charity" and any balance in hand was transferred to the "St. Osyth Almshouse Charity". These almshouses in Clacton Road date from the 17th century and over the years their condition had deteriorated badly. In 1933 however, a lady named Mary Piggott left a bequest of some £11,000. 0s. 0d. for these almshouses, which enabled some improvements to be made. The Trustees in 1981 then took the sensible decision to amalgamate all three charities under the name of "St. Osyth Almshouses" and by this means were able to put the houses into a complete state of repair.

There are also two almshouses in St. Clairs Road, built in 1934, in memory of Mr. Gilder, one of a well known St. Osyth family in the 19th century, whose descendants are still in business in Clacton. A Mr. Gilder was a maltster with property at the wharf and at one time lived at "Priory Cottage" in Spring road, now known as "The Old House", before moving to Duchess Farm.

This subject cannot be left without quoting an extract from the books of 1872 for a Christmas Dinner for approximately 200 people, as follows:

	£	s.	d.
Mr. Norman, 64½lbs. Beef and Suet:	£2.	11s.	0½d.
Mrs. Norman, 70½lbs. Beef and Suet:	£2.	15s.	10d.
Mrs. Osborne		12s.	4d.
Mr. Demaid, 2 bushels potatoes:		7s.	0d.
20lbs plums and salt:		10s.	1½d.
Mrs. Hurst, 25lbs plums:		12s.	6d.
Mrs. Last, Cooking dinner and bread:	£1.	0s.	4d.
Mrs. Smoothy		8s.	4d.
Mrs. Atkins		6s.	0d.
TOTAL	£9.	3s.	6d.

Members of the Norman family were, of course, butchers at that time and Mr. Norman was also a vet., or horse doctor as they were then called. There is no reason to suppose that the two occupations were ever confused!

If the inclusion of plums seems unusual, it should be remembered that in those days they were included in the pudding with the meat and potatoes. One would imagine that a good time was had by all!

Old Almshouses in Clacton Road.

OLD AND LISTED BUILDINGS IN ST. OSYTH

The Department of the Environment has issued a list, revised up to 1986, of buildings or other items of special architectural or historic interest. The list for St. Osyth includes no less than 91 properties or items, some of which are described below. They range from village pumps to a milestone and a pair of ornamental urns at a local farm.

It is obvious that parts of the Priory and the church are the oldest remains in the village but there are many buildings which are centuries old. One which immediately comes to mind is St. Clere's Hall, parts of which have been radio–carbon dated to around 1350. It is a magnificent building, still surrounded by a moat, and it was here that the unfortunate 'witch', Ursula Kemp, was interrogated. Over the later centuries various alterations and additions have been made and this is true of course of almost all properties in the village. Many of these are much older than can be deduced at first glance, as they are built on extremely ancient foundations which are not always to be seen without excavation.

St. Clere's Hall was held under the Earls of Oxford in the reign of Henry III by Ralph, the son of Walter de Osith. Later, in 1273, it was the home of William St. Clere. It continued in the St. Clere family up to 1555, when John St. Clere passed the manor and lands to a John Gason. It then passed to one of the Darcy family.

A house of approximately the same age, or possibly even slightly older, is in Spring Road, now known as 'The Old House', formerly 'Priory Cottage'.

On left Priory Cottage now The Old House. Chestnut House in back-ground

This house, which is now two dwellings, dates from circa 1300 with 15th century and later alterations and additions. The cellar is regarded as being of great interest, with a brick lining being possibly the second earliest example of a brick structure known in Essex after Coggeshall Abbey. It contains a 'Bee bole' which consists of a niche in the wall where a skip would be placed for bees. This is a reminder of the days when honey was the only method of sweetening available.

At one time 'Priory Cottage' was occupied by a Mr. Gilder, who was a maltster with premises at the quay. Later it became the home of Mrs. Cowley. Originally it had a dairy at the rear but now there is only a very large pump in the garden which is on the Environment's List.

It would not be possible to speak of each individual house in this booklet, but it can be broadly stated that the houses and shops gathered around the cross roads at Bar Corner, turning into Spring Road and Colchester Road, are many hundreds of years old. The café on the corner was formerly 'The Ship Inn' and before that 'The Hoy' (a type of ship). It is obvious that ship's timbers and ribs were used in the building of these premises and the adjacent stores, formerly Brett's. The Department of the Environment give a date of the 15th century, but it is highly likely that it is of much earlier origin.

Old houses in Colchester Road, Falcon Inn sign may just be seen at Binders—middle left.

'Binders' in Colchester Road, was an ale house known as 'The Falcon' in about 1910. Up until recently there was a large iron ring in a rear outbuilding, to which tradition relates that either a bull was tethered or a performing bear, which toured the country with a small band of entertainers.

Colchester Road and the lower half of Mill Street have dwellings dating back to earlier centuries with most of them having had structural changes made in later times. 'Ivy Cottage' in Colchester Road and numbers 36 and 38, which were formerly one house, have been dated back to about 1500, while others vary from the 17th, 18th and 19th centuries.

"The Ship Inn—now a Restaurant"

The village houses clustered around the church and Spring Road is rich in old properties for about a hundred yards although, sadly, some have had to be demolished. The butcher's shop on the corner is dated 1784 on the gable but the rear portion dates from the 17th century. The Post Office was in this building, with Mrs. Kath Norman (formerly a Demaid) in charge for many years, after the last war. The Duke Stores and the adjacent cottages are dated to the 16th century or earlier, with later additions and alterations. 'Chestnut Cottage' with two other integral cottages date from the 17th century and at one time a Mr. Demaid, whose ancestor was a carpenter in 1780, lived here when the family had become well known as builders. One of his female descendants married a Mr. Norman, whose family founded the building firm in Clacton Road.

The row of cottages and the baker's shop, which was formerly a house and has another listed pump behind it, date from the late 14th or early 15th centuries. To the right and rear of the present Post Office is a property called 'Cranfield' with adjoining cottages. These pose an intriguing problem. According to the Department of the Environment, one was known as 'The White Hart' in or about 1760. This is interesting as the present 'White Hart Inn' is dated 18th to 19th centuries as to the front range and earlier at the rear. I have seen a Deed dated 15 January 1780 for the lease of 'The White Hart' to Shadrack Seaman (described as a carpenter) from John Bawtree and witnessed by Wm. Genery, in which water rights are mentioned. This surely places the inn near to the quay. We know that on 24 June 1777, a singing competition took place at the inn and it might appear possible that the old inn was closed and a new one opened in its present location soon after 1760.

The 'White Hart' has been mentioned. Two other inns, the 'King's Arms' and the 'Red Lion' both date from at least the 16th century. A fourth, the 'Flag Inn', formerly known as the 'Union Flag', dates from the 18th century whilst the 'Queen's Head', described as a 'beerhouse' was demolished in 1910 to make room for the Johnson Institute. There were several other ale or beerhouses in the village but I have not been able to definitely place their location, other than 'Binders' in Colchester Road and the 'Duke's Head', now the Duke's Stores in Spring Road.

Two cottages in Daltes Lane are worthy of mention as they comprised the old Parish Poor House, being originally known as the 'Tan Cottages'. They were purchased by the Parish in the latter part of the 18th century and were sold to the Tendring Guardians in 1839 soon after the Poor Law Acts were amended.

Not all buildings need to be listed to deserve attention. The Almshouses in Clacton Road are several hundreds of years old. Much later in date, but of great importance and interest, is the Methodist Chapel built in 1853. This must have replaced an earlier place of meeting as an Ecclesiastical Survey in 1841 gives the number of "dissenters" (who would be Wesleyans at that time) as 300. It is not certain where this earlier meeting place was, but there may be a clue in a document conveying property in Spring Road from the widow of William Genery, Schoolmaster, to James Dunnett on 17 May 1834. This comprised "The Chapel House, now used as cottages in Spring Road". These cottages were demolished in fairly recent times, to make way for Barclays Bank and are remembered by many villagers. It could be that this was the original meeting place of the Wesleyans, and before that was the Academy and school conducted by William Genery and then later by Sam Crampin, as mentioned in the chapter on education.

There is a building in Colchester Road which was a chapel in 1841, the home of a religious community known as the Swedenborgians, who had a congregation of 200 and later became known as the New Church.

The local farms are all of ancient origin, the sites dating back to Norman times and presumably even earlier. The actual buildings mainly date from the 15th or 16th centuries, although Park Farm is thought to be of the 14th century period. This had a painted panel which is now in Colchester Museum and there are also wall paintings, which have been carefully covered to avoid deterioration. This farm was one of two parks of the old Priory estate and was known as "The Great Park". The other park was Warren Farm.

On a military aspect, St. Osyth had three Martello Towers, one at Colne Point which is still standing, another, now demolished, on Beacon Heights and one at Jaywick. These were built in the early 1800's, during the Napoleonic wars to repel invasion and a record once hung inside the Colne Point Tower stating that just over one million bricks were required to build each one and furthermore, each exterior brick was curved to the shape of the tower. The entrance was high up on the first floor with a well in the lower level.

As in most villages there have been rumours of "secret" tunnels that are supposed to exist between buildings such as the Priory, the church and St. Clere's Hall. Apart from the obvious problems in keeping such tunnels "secret", the difficulty of construction would be immense, even today, and the necessity for them being even more questionable. It is possible however, and indeed almost certain, that hiding places were constructed for the storage of contraband and these may have been mistaken for the entrance to tunnels. Larger properties had pits and short tunnels which were filled with ice, packed in straw, during the winter and these acted as cold stores throughout the summer months.

"New for Old. Ancient cottages in Mill Street after renovation—note listed pump".

ACKNOWLEDGEMENTS

I must record my indebtedness to Mr. Andrew Smith of Wigboro Wick whose forebears have farmed in the locality for some hundreds of years. It was he who finally urged me to write this story and who has been of great assistance in local matters. I have already mentioned Mr. A. J. Brown of Colchester who was responsible for creating my initial interest and am grateful to Mr. Kenneth Walker for his encouragement and help on some points. Miss Phyll Hendy, the present Parish Council Chairman, has provided various pieces of information, as have several of the older residents of the village. Mr. Brian Tuley and Mr. Ken Clow immediately offered any required photographs from their very extensive collections, the latter willingly making black and white copies of old sepia prints for better reproduction. Tendring Council kindly provided details of listed properties, alas, far too long to be included in this book.

Lastly my thanks go to my daughter Pamela and grand–daughter Debbie, who have typed and re–typed my original drafts and to my long suffering wife, who has had to endure rooms strewn with papers and who will be delighted that this should now cease.

Lawrence A. Foxen.

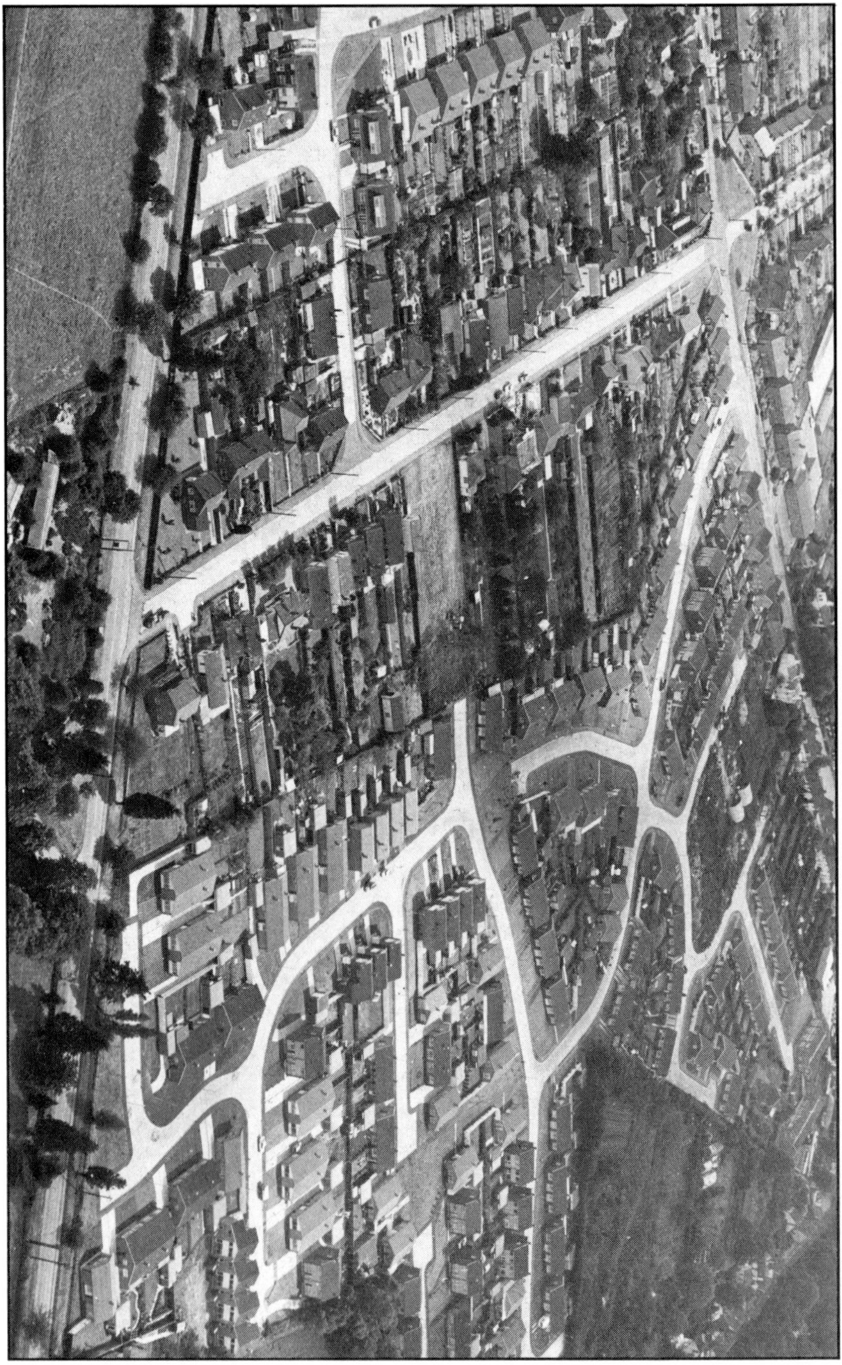

"The old order changeth, giving place to new"